The Retire[illegible]

Stephen Smith

ISBN: 978-1-959392-82-8

Dedication

I have had many mentors, but my parents have made the biggest difference in my life. People in the industry who have helped me grow and succeed are Bill Atkins, Brian Atkins, Mike Dressander, John McDermott, Andy Robertson, and Patrick Wehrly. Without these people, I would not have gone down the path I did.

Hard work does pay off, but everyone needs a little help and guidance to make it through to the end.

Contents

About the Author

Stephen Smith is an Electrical/Computer Engineer who graduated from Marquette University. Engineers make great financial advisors, given how they are trained to think and how analytical they are.

Stephen started in the financial world by trading commodities and helping farmers hedge their corn and soybean crops. His knowledge stems from years of experience working with family farms and was especially utilized during 2008 when the stock and housing markets crashed. Farmers did very well in this environment as land values, corn prices, and soybean prices went through the roof. But they needed a lot of help with finance, tax, investment, and estate planning, which served as a window for Stephen to bring his expertise forward.

This book is everything he has learned throughout the years, and he hopes it can help bring a change in the world of financial planning.

Introduction

The purpose of writing this book was to help you, my reader, plan for the most important part of your retirement. *The Retirement Paycheck* mainly consists of social security, pension, and savings. It is often referred to as the three-legged stool. This book will help you understand that utilizing a proper social security strategy is important as, on average, social security makes up approximately 40% of your retirement income need. Moreover, pensions are being reduced, but many retirees today do have some defined benefits that will add to their monthly cash flow. The main focus of this book will be on savings, generally from 401ks, IRAs, and cash.

My firm, Significant Wealth Partners, is a registered investment advisory firm (RIA). People meet with us after attending one of our live workshops (usually my workshop on social security, but we discuss other topics as well), and we usually deal with providing a solution to problems related to cash flow. After discussing how social security, at different stages, impacts the overall retirement plan, we then come up with a plan to fill in the gap. The gap is the difference between what social security and pension contribute to your budget. The savings component is then used to solve this gap, and there are multiple ways to do it. This book will take a deep dive into those strategies and hopefully clear up some misconceptions.

Many people rely on the 4% rule, which simply states that if you withdraw 4% of your money from your savings each year, you "should" have enough money. The reason behind this strategy is that the market averages 8%/year, or so it is said. The market will "always come back," and I firmly believe in that. However, retirement is different since you are no longer contributing money to your savings accounts, like 401ks and IRAs. Will you retire at the start of a good market or a bad one? You don't know the answer to this question, and neither do I. Nonetheless, I will discuss the sequence of return risk and how it impacts the 4% rule.

The second part of *The Retirement Paycheck* is focused on making it as tax-efficient as possible. In my workshops, I always ask how many people think income tax rates will go lower. I have never had anyone raise their hand. As a matter of fact, it usually gets a chuckle out of all of the attendees. This book will show you how to minimize the impact of taxation in your retirement. You have to remember that, for most of you, the majority of your savings are in your 401k and IRA (tax-deferred). You owe taxes on this money, and every dollar you take out will be taxed at your ordinary income rate. Your tax-deferred IRA could have $2 million in it, but that $2 million is NOT all yours. A good chunk of that money belongs to the IRS. It's THEIRS; you should spell it out: The I R S.

Lastly, I will touch on some other areas of retirement planning. I meet a lot of people who don't have a basic estate plan; not everyone needs a trust, but you do need a will. I will discuss some estate planning basics as well as Medicare and Long-Term Care, as these are two very important topics for retirees.

Don't be afraid to take notes as you go through this book, and if any questions come up, you can always send us an email at info@swp360.com. I also have a YouTube channel with educational videos on most of the topics that are covered in this book; https://www.youtube.com/channel/UCORpvlh5kC5p9Dzatcmev5A Please subscribe to the channel, it's free. Turn on the notification bell so that you are updated when a new video comes out.

Let's begin!!

Chapter 1: Retirement Is Different

If you had retired in the early 1980s, your retirement plan would have been built a lot differently from how we build them today. You see, back in the early 1980s, bank Certificates of Deposits, commonly called CDs, were paying 8, 10, and 12%, and you were able to earn a significant income just by keeping your money in CDs. I can't think of a single place to invest money in today where you can earn a guaranteed 8, 10, and 12%.[1] Think about that, if you had $1 million in a bank CD, paying 12%, that would equal $120,000 in interest. Take that, plus your social security and pension, and you would have lived a very nice retirement. The good thing is, you would still have your $1 million, as the rest of the $120,000 would have come from interest on the bank CD.

Unfortunately, you can't buy a bank CD paying 12% today. As a matter of fact, you can't buy a bank CD paying even 2%. As of writing this book, I looked up the best CD rates in my area; at that point in time, the top rate was 1.90% for 5 years. If you put $1 million into this bank CD for 5 years, you would earn $19,000/year in interest each year.[2] For most of my clients, that amount will not be enough to

---

[1] https://www.bankrate.com/banking/cds/historical-cd-interest-rates/#:~:text=CD%20rates%20in%20the%201980s&text=On%20average%2C%20three%2Dmonth%20CDs,doesn't%20buy%20as%20much.

[2] https://www.bankrate.com/banking/cds/cd-calculator/

fill the gap between social security, pension, and the actual budget needed. The other issue with these low rates is inflation; social security had a 5.9% increase going from 2021 into 2022. This is the highest COLA (Cost-of-living Adjustment) we have seen from social security in quite some time.[3] Moreover, Medicare part B had a 14% increase going into 2022,[4] meaning the 1.9% bank CD isn't going to be enough as your Retirement Paycheck needs to keep up with inflation.

When the 2008 financial crisis occurred, the Federal Reserve dropped interest rates as they needed to stimulate the economy; this is called Monetary Policy, where the Fed controls the money supply to either jump-start the economy (lowering interest rates) or tame inflation (raising interest rates). When interest rates are lowered, the government doesn't provide the people with the opportunity to save money as they give you no incentive to do so with low rates. These low rates also provide easy access to capital for a business, allowing it to hire resources, market, and expand its operations. With low-interest rates, the housing market was able to come back quickly after 2008, as you could get a 30-year mortgage rate between 3.50 and 4%.[5] Some of you

---

3 https://www.cnbc.com/2022/03/10/inflation-may-boost-social-security-cost-of-living-adjustment-in-2023.html#:~:text=In%20comparison%2C%20the%20Social%20Security,over%20the%20past%2012%20months.

4 https://www.cnbc.com/2021/11/12/medicare-standard-part-b-premiums-for-2022-jump-by-14point5percent-.html

5 https://themortgagereports.com/61853/30-year-mortgage-rates-chart

probably remember the 1980s when your first mortgage had a 15-20% interest rate, yikes!

Due to low-interest rates, savers were not rewarded and had to find another way to earn interest on their money. The answer for many individual investors, then, was the stock market. From March of 2009 through December of 2021, the S&P 500 averaged 17.35% per year if you reinvested the dividends.[6] Let's put this another way: If you had invested $100,000 in March of 2009, the approximate value of your investment by December 2021 would have been over $800,000. Over the last 13 years, the stock market has provided many with the greatest creation of wealth ever seen in this country.

Most people feel that if their money is doubling every 10 years, they are doing well. I do agree with this as it means your money would average 7.2% per year for 10 years; I don't think anyone would complain about that - this also puts into perspective how good the stock market has been since March of 2009. As a matter of fact, most people seem to forget that the market can go even lower. When we were all quarantined, and the world was shut down due to COVID-19, the market had a 34% top to bottom drop (The S&P 500).[7] It was quite the scare for many, but if you had taken the long-term approach, your money would have recovered very quickly. For the year

---

6 https://www.macrotrends.net/2324/sp-500-historical-chart-data

7 https://www.statista.com/statistics/1175227/s-and-p-500-major-crashes-change/

2020, the S&P closed up 17%, making the earlier drop of 34% in February and March appear like it never happened.

Sequence of Return Risk

As strong as the stock market has been, we have to build retirement plans differently. I believe in two things when it comes to the stock market:

1. The best stock market we have ever seen is still in front of us.

2. The worst stock market we have ever seen is still in front of us.

You have to build retirement plans to account for the worst-case scenario. You need your Retirement Paycheck to be there whether the market goes up or down. I like to use the "lost decade" as a way of building Retirement Paychecks; from January 2000 through December of 2009, the S&P 500, with dividends reinvested, averaged -1.98% per year.[6] Below is a chart that will help you understand this concept had you retired on January 1st, 2000. The S&P performance shows, with dividends being reinvested and taking $40,000 withdrawals, increasing at 2%/year due to inflation. We are starting with a 1% management fee, which is why you see the net growth after the management fee. We are also assuming a $1 million investment into the

S&P 500. The chart will show you how a 4% distribution rate using the S&P 500 can fail.

The $1 million invested by the end of 2009 is worth $376,011. Retirees, in my experience, don't want to see their nest eggs draw down. This becomes pretty scary as there are so many unexpected expenses that can occur in retirement. Watching your assets go down in value due to distributions and poor market performance can cause panic to anyone. Also, the 2% increase due to inflation may not be enough in today's inflationary environment. The reason the money is being drawn down is that you are forced to sell shares of what you own to generate the $40,000 in income. The dividends provided by the S&P are not enough to cover the $40,000 income needed.

GROWTH BUCKET	S&P 500	Net Growth	Income	Account Balance
2000	-9.10%	-10.10%	$40,000	$859,000.00
2001	-11.89%	-12.89%	$40,800	$707,474.90
2002	-22.10%	-23.10%	$41,616	$502,432.20
2003	28.68%	27.68%	$42,448	$599,057.11
2004	10.88%	9.88%	$43,297	$614,946.67
2005	4.91%	3.91%	$44,163	$594,827.85
2006	15.79%	14.79%	$45,046	$637,756.39
2007	5.49%	4.49%	$45,947	$620,444.23
2008	-37.00%	-38.00%	$46,866	$337,809.05
2009	26.46%	25.46%	$47,804	$376,011.53

Figure 1

Below is the exact same chart showing no income need or distribution from the $1 million investment. When you don't take money out, as you can see by the ending value of $819,084, your money does start to recover. The question is, will you retire at the beginning of a strong stock market or a weak one? This is an impossible question to answer which is why you should not have your retirement plan based on what the overall stock market is doing.

GROWTH BUCKET	S&P 500	Net Growth	Income	Account Balance
2000	-9.10%	-10.10%	$0	$899,000.00
2001	-11.89%	-12.89%	$0	$783,118.90
2002	-22.10%	-23.10%	$0	$602,218.43
2003	28.68%	27.68%	$0	$768,912.50
2004	10.88%	9.88%	$0	$844,881.05
2005	4.91%	3.91%	$0	$877,915.90
2006	15.79%	14.79%	$0	$1,007,759.66
2007	5.49%	4.49%	$0	$1,053,008.07
2008	-37.00%	-38.00%	$0	$652,865.00
2009	26.46%	25.46%	$0	$819,084.43

Figure 2

Having a reliable paycheck in retirement is very important, and you can now understand the problem with relying on stock market growth. It's great when the growth is there, but it can be devastating to your retirement if it's not. Unfortunately, there is not a single financial advisor in the world that can control the stock market. We don't know when the stock market will go up or when it will underperform. As a financial advisor, I feel the stock market will go up over time; however, we have to build plans to get through the bad times, as those will surely come.

When people come to our office after one of our workshops, the first thing I look at on their statements is income. I ask them, 'How do you plan to take money out of this account when you retire?' Unfortunately, not one person has been able to answer that question. They usually tell me they leave it to their advisor. Here, I am going to encourage you not to leave anything to your advisor. Your advisor should be providing the knowledge and expertise, but you should be the one making the decisions. A 4% distribution rule on your money can fail if we end up in bad markets. The conservative part of your portfolio, bond funds, could make it a worse failure if we do see inflation and rising interest rates.

Bond Funds

Bond funds have always been looked at as more conservative. When people approach retirement, the majority of the time, they want to be more conservative as they don't want to lose a portion of what they have worked so hard to accumulate. You don't want your 401k to become a 201k right when you are about to retire. For the last 40 years, bonds have been looked at as a more conservative investment, and truthfully, they have been just that. The reason is that the interest rates have come down since the

1980s. Below is a chart of the 10-year treasury from CNBC.com that illustrates what interest rates have done going back 40 years.[8]

Figure 3

As of writing this book, the 10-year treasury is at 2.45% (March 28th, 2022). Below is a different look at the exact same image as above. However, the data range starts in January of 2020, just before the COVID-19 pandemic started.[8] You can see that the interest rates changed very quickly once the pandemic started as the whole world went into quarantine.

[8] https://www.cnbc.com/quotes/US10Y

Figure 4

In March of 2020, interest rates fell quickly and stayed low through the remainder of the year, as illustrated on the left side of the above chart. As the pandemic raged on, we started to have problems in the supply chain; restaurants, retail and more businesses became very understaffed. The government printed a lot of money to flood the economy to avert disaster. This is what created the problem we have today, which is inflation. The way the government counters inflation is by raising interest rates. In the above chart, you can see interest rates, since reaching the bottom in July of 2020, have come up significantly. Interest rates are expected to continue to rise as the FED has announced they will be raising rates quite a few times in 2022 (still unknown how many times). The conservative part of your portfolio may not remain as conservative as you once thought.

Keep in mind that there is a difference between owning an individual bond and a bond fund. I am going to focus on bond funds, as that is what most people own in their portfolios today. Yes, a bond fund does consist of all individual bonds, and they all have a duration attached to them, which refers to the average duration of the holdings in the fund. If a bond fund has a duration of 10 years, it means the average length of the holdings within the fund comes due in 10 years. Individual bonds typically mature at par value. For example, if you put $100,000 into an individual bond, paying 5% for 10 years, you will receive the 5% in interest every year, and at the end of 10 years, you will receive your $100,000 back. Still, there are some risks associated with individual bonds. For instance, people might have to reinvest proceeds at a lower rate than what the funds were previously earning.[9] Similarly, they might face default risk, which means that the bond's issuer might not be able to make timely payments causing the investor to lose part of or all of the investment. If one invests in corporate bonds, the original investment can be at risk if the company collapses or goes into bankruptcy.

Bond funds work a little differently, and I will do my best to keep this simple. If interest rates rise, as they are today, the value of your principal in a bond fund drops. And if the interest rates go down, then the value of your principal rises. Figure 3 shows the 10-year treasury going down the last 40

---

9 https://www.investopedia.com/articles/bonds/08/bond-risks.asp

years, which means the value of your principal, depending on when you bought them, has gone up. This year, in 2022, the value of your principal has gone down as interest rates have started to rise. It's just that simple.

So, what has worked for the last 40 years may not be so beneficial in the coming years. This is why I feel the 60/40 portfolio, which consists of 60% equity exposure and 40% bond exposure, is dead. I can't predict the stock market or interest rates, but I have concerns about this mix of investments. As it relates to the Retirement Paycheck, there is nothing consistent about generating a paycheck from this type of portfolio. In my experience, the 60/40 portfolio is what most people walk into my office with. This isn't a reliable paycheck in retirement, and you also don't need to pay a financial advisor to buy you a 60/40 portfolio of mutual funds and ETFs. Typically, these portfolios consist of the following components:

1. Large Cap
2. Mid Cap
3. Small Cap
4. International Emerging Markets
5. Bonds – Short-term, intermediate-term, long-term, and high yield

You have to think about the possibility that if the United States raises interest rates, we can get into a situation where your "conservative bond funds" and your stock equities don't perform well at the same time. Yes, this can happen! I worry and wonder if the United States economy can afford higher interest rates since we have a $30 trillion deficit, and every 1% rise in rates will cost us $300 billion in interest payments.[10] Whom do you think will pay that bill?

Raising interest rates will also have an impact on the housing market, businesses, car loans, student loans, and even things beyond that. Can the United States of America afford to increase rates on Americans that are planning to go to college and take out student loans to do it? Can future homeowners afford to pay higher interest rates to buy a house? Can a small business survive with higher interest rates on its loans? The answers to these questions are unknown, but these keep me up at night when thinking about my clients in retirement.

More Fun Data!

Earlier in this chapter, I shared an example of a sequence of return risk showing how a 4% distribution starting at the worst possible time (January 1st, 2000) could cause you to run out of money. I am now going to continue that illustration, showing what happened after that 10-year period. The S&P 500 did very well from 2009 through 2021. I am going to show this for two purposes:

---

[10] https://usdebtclock.org/

1. If you are still working, the long-term approach to investing does still work.

2. If you are retired and taking 4% out per year for income, the long-term approach still doesn't help you recover your money.

The below chart now shows the year 2000 through 2021. We are still taking out the 4% or $40,000 per year and increasing it by 2%/year for inflation.

GROWTH BUCKET	S&P 500	Net Growth	Income	Account Balance
2000	-9.10%	-10.10%	$40,000	$859,000.00
2001	-11.89%	-12.89%	$40,800	$707,474.90
2002	-22.10%	-23.10%	$41,616	$502,432.20
2003	28.68%	27.68%	$42,448	$599,057.11
2004	10.88%	9.88%	$43,297	$614,946.67
2005	4.91%	3.91%	$44,163	$594,827.85
2006	15.79%	14.79%	$45,046	$637,756.39
2007	5.49%	4.49%	$45,947	$620,444.23
2008	-37.00%	-38.00%	$46,866	$337,809.05
2009	26.46%	25.46%	$47,804	$376,011.53
2010	15.06%	14.06%	$48,760	$380,118.97
2011	2.11%	1.11%	$49,735	$334,603.32
2012	16.00%	15.00%	$50,730	$334,064.14
2013	32.39%	31.39%	$51,744	$387,182.61
2014	13.69%	12.69%	$52,779	$383,536.94
2015	1.38%	0.38%	$53,835	$331,159.64
2016	11.96%	10.96%	$54,911	$312,543.31
2017	21.83%	20.83%	$56,010	$321,636.43
2018	-4.38%	-5.38%	$57,130	$247,202.54
2019	31.49%	30.49%	$58,272	$264,302.14
2020	18.40%	17.40%	$59,438	$250,852.82
2021	28.71%	27.71%	$60,627	$259,737.48
Total Income			$1,091,959	

Figure 5

Before I make my point, here is the chart showing the exact same thing but without the distribution needed for income.

GROWTH BUCKET	S&P 500	Net Growth	Income	Account Balance
2000	-9.10%	-10.10%	$0	$899,000.00
2001	-11.89%	-12.89%	$0	$783,118.90
2002	-22.10%	-23.10%	$0	$602,218.43
2003	28.68%	27.68%	$0	$768,912.50
2004	10.88%	9.88%	$0	$844,881.05
2005	4.91%	3.91%	$0	$877,915.90
2006	15.79%	14.79%	$0	$1,007,759.66
2007	5.49%	4.49%	$0	$1,053,008.07
2008	-37.00%	-38.00%	$0	$652,865.00
2009	26.46%	25.46%	$0	$819,084.43
2010	15.06%	14.06%	$0	$934,247.71
2011	2.11%	1.11%	$0	$944,617.85
2012	16.00%	15.00%	$0	$1,086,310.53
2013	32.39%	31.39%	$0	$1,427,303.41
2014	13.69%	12.69%	$0	$1,608,428.21
2015	1.38%	0.38%	$0	$1,614,540.24
2016	11.96%	10.96%	$0	$1,791,493.85
2017	21.83%	20.83%	$0	$2,164,662.02
2018	-4.38%	-5.38%	$0	$2,048,203.20
2019	31.49%	30.49%	$0	$2,672,700.36
2020	18.40%	17.40%	$0	$3,137,750.22
2021	28.71%	27.71%	$0	$4,007,220.81
Total Income			$0	

Figure 6

Do you see the difference? In the first chart, when you are taking out the $40,000/year increasing at 2% for inflation, you have $259,737 left. You spent $1,091,959 over this period, as that is the total for the distributions. If you had not needed the income and taken no money out over this same time period, you would now have $4,007,220. I know it sounds crazy, but it's true! I hope you can now see why I say that retirement is different in present times.

For those still working with a long-time horizon before retirement, the above illustration represents the point that you don't need to be the smartest investor in the world to achieve strong results. You don't need to beat the S&P, as just being the S&P can lead to financial independence. The below chart shows $100,000 invested into the S&P 500 over the same time period and making additions to the investment each year (assuming this is a 401k type investment).

GROWTH BUCKET	S&P 500	Net Growth	Annual Additions	Account Balance
2000	-9.10%	-10.10%	$20,000	$109,900.00
2001	-11.89%	-12.89%	$20,000	$115,733.89
2002	-22.10%	-23.10%	$20,000	$108,999.36
2003	28.68%	27.68%	$20,000	$159,170.38
2004	10.88%	9.88%	$20,000	$194,896.42
2005	4.91%	3.91%	$20,000	$222,516.87
2006	15.79%	14.79%	$20,000	$275,427.11
2007	5.49%	4.49%	$20,000	$307,793.79
2008	-37.00%	-38.00%	$20,000	$210,832.15
2009	26.46%	25.46%	$20,000	$284,510.02
2010	15.06%	14.06%	$20,000	$344,512.12
2011	2.11%	1.11%	$20,000	$368,336.21
2012	16.00%	15.00%	$20,000	$443,586.64
2013	32.39%	31.39%	$20,000	$602,828.49
2014	13.69%	12.69%	$20,000	$699,327.42
2015	1.38%	0.38%	$20,000	$721,984.87
2016	11.96%	10.96%	$20,000	$821,114.41
2017	21.83%	20.83%	$20,000	$1,012,152.54
2018	-4.38%	-5.38%	$20,000	$977,698.73
2019	31.49%	30.49%	$20,000	$1,295,799.07
2020	18.40%	17.40%	$20,000	$1,541,268.11
2021	28.71%	27.71%	$20,000	$1,988,353.51
Total Additions			$440,000	

Figure 7

It truly is amazing what compound interest can do over time; had the additions not been made, the $100k would have turned into $400,722.

Important information from chapter 1:

1. Understand the Sequence of Return Risk and how it can impact your retirement when you have to sell shares of the assets you own.
2. Bond Funds may not be as conservative in the future due to a rise in interest rates.
3. Your Retirement Paycheck needs to be prepared for both good and bad markets.

Chapter 2: Building the Retirement Paycheck

The Retirement Paycheck is how we solve the sequence of return risk and rising interest rates. We have to design a cash flow retirement plan that works regardless of interest rates and stock market performance. It needs to be reliable in all scenarios. There are no 'one size fits all' answers to this, and the solution will need consistent updating and work. Nothing in this world is "GUARANTEED," and I mean nothing. Many of you are sold on annuities that provide "GUARANTEED" income. However, that income is only guaranteed against the claims-paying ability of the insurance company. I am not against annuities, but I don't like it when the salesperson says the word "GUARANTEED." Life is unpredictable, so you can't put all of your eggs into one basket. I know many of you have heard about diversification, but in retirement, diversification is the key to avoid disaster.[11]

In my opinion, a large amount of wealth isn't usually created by diversification. I have met with a lot of individuals, who have accumulated over $10 million in investable assets, and it's not because they diversified. Many times, it's because they sold their business. I am ok

---

11 https://www.investopedia.com/terms/d/diversification.asp

with this type of wealth creation as it's your life's work that created the wealth. Other times, I have also come across people who come in, owning 1 or 2 stocks that did well. I've even met with people who had all of their money invested in Abbott and AbbVie stock, Tesla stock, Apple stock, and FANG (Facebook, Amazon, Netflix, and Google). Now, I am certainly not saying that these were, or are, bad choices; what I am saying is that they don't provide consistent and reliable income.[12] I am a big believer that trees don't grow to the sky. A great example of this would be GE stock; many of my older clients held a large position in GE, which was not due to my recommendation, and for many years, GE was a great stock to own until it wasn't. Your retirement plan needs to account for the unknown. I always like to say, "We don't know what we don't know." You can absolutely hold those individual stocks that have helped you create wealth. However, should you continue to have all of your money there? I can't answer that question for you, but I am going to talk about a diversified plan that provides consistent income, safety, and growth. You can have it all if you want it, but there is a cost, as your money will not grow the way the previously mentioned stocks have. I believe diversification with the proper income, safety, and growth portfolio is a great medicine for sleeping at night.

---

[12] https://www.investopedia.com/ask/answers/12/why-do-some-companies-pay-a-dividend.asp

Dividends

Let's start designing the Retirement Paycheck. The first topic that I will be discussing is dividends. Honestly, it is my favorite way to generate consistent and reliable income in retirement. First off, most of the people that I meet with have already used the stock market to create the money they had saved for retirement. The old saying, "If it ain't broke, don't fix it," comes to mind as the stock market has put you in the position you are in today. So, how do we utilize stock market vehicles to generate a Retirement Paycheck? The answer is dividends![13]

Let's start with how dividends actually work. I am going to give you a very specific example of Verizon Communications (Verizon Wireless) stock to explain how dividends work. I am only using this to help you understand how dividends work. The ticker symbol for Verizon is VZ, and if you google "VZ," Verizon's common stock information comes up. Verizon is $51.17/share as of writing this (March 28th, 2022), and Verizon currently pays a dividend of $2.56/share. If you purchased $100,000 worth of Verizon, you would buy 1,954 shares ($100,000 divided by the share price of $51.17). Verizon pays

[13]https://www.simplysafedividends.com/intelligent-income/posts/1-living-off-dividends-in-retirement

$2.56/share for every share you own, which equals an annual dividend paycheck of $5,002.

Now, let's say Verizon's share price gets cut in half to $25.58/share. This means your $100,000 investment just turned into $50,000. Many people think the dividend would also get cut in half. However, this isn't the case. You still owned 1,954 shares when the stock price fell - that didn't change. Next, as long as Verizon didn't cut the $2.56 dividend they are paying per share, you would still receive $5,002 in annual income. Many people feel that when the stock price falls, companies automatically reduce the dividend. Dividends can be reduced, which is why you don't put all of your eggs into one basket.

Many times, share prices fall due to a 'panic.' I include 2008 and March of 2020 under this banner when the whole world went into a lockdown and was quarantined. Panics, in my experience, don't cause dividends to get cut. Those companies are still in business, but due to what is happening around the world, investors have started selling their shares, causing the stock price to fall. Panics don't scare me anymore, as I now see them as opportunities. But what scares me is when someone has all of their money in a few holdings. I understand there are a lot of good companies out there, but, as I said before, they are good until they are not, and GE is a perfect example of that. Retirement is about spreading out that risk; if you are still trying to create wealth in retirement, do it with the money you don't need for income. The first thing we need a solution for is cash flow. Meaning, how much will your social security generate, how much pension you will receive, and then how much of your assets do we need to use to fill the gap? You don't need to have all of your money-generating income (I will touch upon this in further chapters).

Coming back to our discussion, the key to success with a dividend portfolio is to spread out the risk over thousands of positions. By doing this, you have accounted for the unknown, that is, with a dividend portfolio, dividends getting cut. By spreading that risk out over thousands of positions, you minimize the overall impact on your portfolio when those positions cut their dividends.[14] Similarly, you also need to update the portfolio to replace stocks that reduce their dividends. My company, Significant Wealth Partners, has designed three income portfolios to help you go from your work paycheck to your Retirement Paycheck and these portfolios are very well diversified. The goal of the income portfolio is to generate a consistent paycheck and keep your principal. If the portfolio is paying 5% on $1 Million over a 10-year period, you will generate $500,000 in income or $50,000/year. If you still have the $1 Million at the end of 10 years, the portfolio would have accomplished its goal. It could even be higher than the $1 Million, or it could be lower, but the

[14] https://time.com/nextadvisor/investing/how-dividend-stocks-work/

goal is the consistency of the $50,000 in income per year. Again, most of you don't need all of your money-generating income. I will discuss how to generate growth on top of income later in the book, and I think you will really like this strategy! Growth in the overall portfolio is very important as it relates to increasing your dividend income to keep up with inflation over time. (If you want to learn more about our portfolios, you can send a request email to info@swp360.com)

Let's take another look at the sequence of return example I gave in Chapter 1, where the $1 Million investment is distributed 4%/year, for income inflating at 2%/year. In that example, the $1 Million turned into $259,737, and you got to spend $1,091,959 over the years, from 2000 through 2021. This occurred because the S&P doesn't generate enough dividend income, and the shares needed to be sold to generate $40k/year in income and grow for inflation every year, which means more shares would need to be sold to keep up. If the income needs were being covered by the dividends, then you wouldn't have had to sell the shares. You would most likely still have the $1 Million (highly probable that you would have a lot more than $1 Million as there is some growth with an income portfolio) and still got to spend the $1,091,959.

This is why the dividend approach is my favorite way to generate retirement income, as you're not giving up your money if you do it properly.[15] I am going to talk about annuities next, and the problem I have with annuities (that provide a guaranteed paycheck) is that you give up the money. With the dividend approach, you don't give up the money if you do it properly. Now, you do need to know that generating dividend income takes a lot of work. This approach is not like buying a large-cap mutual fund where you can just park your money there for 20 years. With a dividend portfolio, you need to manage, rebalance, and update those positions. It needs constant attention as things do move and change. A dividend portfolio purchased in the year 2000 would be very different from a dividend portfolio today.

By now, you have learned that a portfolio with dividend-paying stocks isn't a bad way to generate a Retirement Paycheck. However, you should diversify outside of stocks as well. Our portfolios are very well diversified as stocks are not the only investments in them. I could make this entire book about positions that pay dividends, but most of you just want a diversified portfolio that works and pays a consistent Retirement Paycheck. Hence, I will not go into more detail on other components, but just know there are other components in the portfolios that make up the Retirement Paycheck.

---

[15] https://www.thebalance.com/making-money-from-dividends-357434

Annuities

Let's talk about annuities now. I like to tell a joke whenever I end my workshops. It goes: if you want to manage your retirement budget, move to the state of Florida, and you can have breakfast, lunch, and dinner with a financial advisor trying to sell you an annuity. Financial advisors consider annuities to be very popular investment vehicles to generate a Retirement Paycheck. The word "guaranteed" seems to come up a lot with annuities. I don't like the word "guaranteed," as the paycheck is only guaranteed up to the claims-paying ability of the insurance company.[16] Now, I am not saying that annuities are bad; what I am saying is that they are misrepresented by many financial advisors trying to earn high commissions.

I am going to, as simply as I can, help you understand the world of annuities. The first thing you need to know is that there are four main types of annuities, and we are going to talk about each one.

Immediate Annuity

The first type of annuity is an immediate annuity. Think of it as social security, although that would be a deferred immediate annuity, as you have paid into social security

---

16 https://insight.factset.com/when-analyzing-insurance-companies-theres-more-to-ratings-than-meets-the-eye#:~:text=Credit%20Rating%20vs.&text=Some%20analysts%20call%20this%20the,%2C%20Fitch%2C%20or%20Kroll%20Ratings.

your whole working life, resulting in a paycheck from the federal government. The money you paid into social security can't be accessed by you, but the monthly paycheck can be accessed as early as age 62 (not accounting for disability) and taken as late as age 70.[17] If you take social security at age 66 and die one year later, there is no lump-sum payment to your beneficiaries other than the $255 one-time death benefit. What a deal! That money stays in the social security system. And if you are married, your spouse will receive the higher benefit (yours or theirs). They don't, however, receive both benefits. You have to account for this in your income planning, as when one spouse passes away, budgets don't get cut in half, and you will need a solution to make up that gap of a lost social security benefit.

The immediate annuity works similar to social security as you give the insurance company a lump-sum investment. In return, you receive a monthly paycheck that is guaranteed for life. When you die, there is no beneficiary; however, you can set up the annuity to cover a spouse by taking the joint payout option. You can also select certain period options if the insurance company offers them.[18]

---

[17] https://www.ssa.gov/benefits/retirement/planner/agereduction.html#:~:text=Starting%20Your%20Retirement%20Benefits%20Early,reach%20your%20full%20retirement%20age.

[18] https://www.kiplinger.com/article/insurance/t003-c000-s001-create-a-paycheck-with-an-annuity.html#:~:text=An%20immediate%20annuity%20guara

Another word to describe an immediate annuity is annuitization. This is a keyword as the insurance company is annuitizing the payments over your life expectancy. If you live a long life, you beat the insurance company, but if you die young, the insurance company wins and keeps your money.[19]

I am not a fan of the immediate annuity as I don't like the idea of giving up money to the insurance company. You don't know when you will die, and I don't want the insurance company to keep your money in the end. There are better people or places to leave your money to when you pass away. On top of that, the paycheck coming from the immediate annuity doesn't keep up with inflation. It will provide a consistent paycheck, kind of like a pension, but the income will not increase. What happens is that, over time, your purchasing power with the immediate annuity diminishes as inflation causes your budget needs to go up.[20] I had an individual meet with me after attending one of my seminars. He had purchased an immediate annuity for 10 years and wanted to fill the gap between his age of 60 and to take social security at 70. He put $300k into an immediate annuity that now paid him $33k per year for 10

---

ntees%20stable,of%20your%20initial%20investment%20annually.

19 https://www.retireguide.com/annuities/annuitization/#:~:text=Annuitization%20is%20the%20process%20of,annuity%20is%20a%20permanent%20decision.

20 https://www.forbes.com/sites/steveparrish/2019/06/17/taming-the-inflation-risk-in-annuity-payouts/?sh=603eccab206c

years. That meant he would receive $330,000 over the 10 years and then have nothing left. He essentially gave up the $300k for an extra $33k over 10 years. I don't consider this to be a good deal.

Variable Annuity

The second type of annuity is the variable annuity. It is simply a variable annuity that allows for non-qualified funds to be invested tax deferred. Now, if you invest IRA money into the variable annuity, then it's already tax-deferred due to the IRA status. The variable annuity generally invests in mutual fund investments, and all you are doing is wrapping an insurance company around investments that you can buy outside of the annuity. Sometimes, there is a benefit to this, especially if you are under the age of 59^1/2, as non-qualified money can grow without tax implications until you take the money out.

However, the tax benefit may not always be a benefit, depending on your tax situation. Gains in the annuity are taxed at ordinary income rates. If you invest that money into the same positions outside of the annuity (again, using non-qualified money), then you would pay capital gains taxes when you sell those investments. The capital gains rate for many could be better than the ordinary income rates. Also, non-qualified money invested outside of the annuity receives a step up on the basis upon death. This means your beneficiaries won't have to pay taxes on the gain you received as they inherit the positions at the value on the date of your death. Annuities don't work this way with non-qualified money, as now the beneficiary has to take the non-qualified inherited stretch option or pay the tax on the gain at ordinary income rates. Non-qualified stretch with an inherited annuity simply means that you are taking a required distribution every year. This allows one to manage the taxes and stretch the inherited annuity over the beneficiary's life expectancy.[21]

Many times, people hear annuities have high fees or hidden fees. In many cases, that statement is correct when describing a variable annuity. Most, not all, variable annuities are sold with an income rider. The income rider guarantees that the annuity, regardless of performance, will provide a guaranteed stream of income at some point down the road for the owner/annuitant or annuitants.[22] (I will discuss the income rider in the later sections as it can be added to other types of annuities as well.) When you call the insurance company and ask about the fees, you need to be specific with your questions. Variable annuities generally have a mortality and expense charge, administration charge, income and or death benefit rider charge, and sub-account charges. Hence, the total cost can

---

[21] https://www.investopedia.com/ask/answers/082715/how-are-nonqualified-variable-annuities-taxed.asp

[22] https://www.annuityexpertadvice.com/annuity-101/income-rider/#:~:text=The%20annuity%20income%20rider%20is,as%20an%20alternative%20to%20annuitization.

range between 3 and 5%/year in charges when you add them all up.[23]

In my experience, the variable annuities I have come across have been more beneficial for the people selling them than the people buying them. Many times, annuity sales come with an illustration showing what the "potential" is for you to invest your money into. I had a prospect come to my office with an illustration that showed had she put money into this variable annuity, dating back to 1987 (using the S&P as the investment choice), she would have been able to withdraw $372,000/year guaranteed for life. This means her $250,000 investment would have grown to just over $9.3 Million over a 35-year time. Now the rider kicks in, guaranteeing her a 4% payout regardless of market performance. I will be honest, looking at this, I am all in! This would be great, and you can sign me up for this every time.

However, this woman was 65 years old and didn't have 35 years of time on her side. And we also don't know if you will be investing the money into the S&P when times are good or bad. The 35-year illustration was based on the S&P's performance over that time period (which was a 10.9% annualized rate of return). You can't base your retirement income on these unknown factors. Had the

23 https://www.investopedia.com/articles/retirement/02/031302.asp#:~:text=Key%20Takeaways,to%20age%2059%C2%BD%2C%20among%20others.

woman retired in the year 2000, expecting to get 10.9%/year from the S&P in her annuity, she would have been very disappointed as the S&P averaged negative 1.98%/year over her first 10 years of the contract.

My point is simple, illustrations are not worth the paper they are printed on. Now, many of the newer variable annuities do come with the guaranteed income rider, which provides either the highest daily value or a roll-up rate to the income account value. This does solve the problem of the unknowns when dealing with the stock market. However, when you start drawing the money out, over time, it is highly probable that you will give up the money that you put in. Many of the income riders had a guaranteed roll-up rate of 7%. When you look at your variable annuity statement, you will see two values; one is the account value which is the actual value of your investment based on the underlining investment choices you are in. The other is the guaranteed minimum withdrawal benefit or living benefit value. This value is used to determine how much annual income you will receive for the rest of your life.[24] It's not a real value as it relates to your money and is mainly used for marketing purposes. Once the rider is turned on, the income account value or living benefit value no longer means anything, as now you are withdrawing money from the account value. So, think about it, you are withdrawing

24 https://www.ubs.com/content/dam/static/wmamericas/Variable_Annuity_Disclosure.pdf

between 5 and 7% of your account value due to the income rider, plus the 3-5% in annual fees plus or minus market gain or losses. You will quickly learn that you can deplete your account value faster than you think. Now, the income payment from the rider will be there even when the account value hits zero, but you just gave up all your money. This is also why I prefer the dividend approach to income planning, as you get the paycheck like the annuity, but you get to keep your money. I will illustrate the concept of the income rider shortly when I discuss the fixed index annuity.

Fixed Annuity

The third type of annuity is a fixed annuity. Think of it as a bank CD, as it has a stated interest rate for a period of time. You can buy a fixed annuity of almost any duration of up to 10 years. I remember back in 2006, you could have purchased a 10-year fixed annuity with a 6% rate guarantee. If your goal was to take out 4% for income, this would have accomplished your goal on top of reinvesting the other 2%, which would increase your income over time. Today, you can't buy a 10-year fixed annuity paying 6%, but that could change if interest rates go up. The main difference between a fixed annuity and a bank CD is that a fixed annuity is tax-deferred, while a bank CD is taxed every year (non-qualified money). In most cases, there are no direct fees with a fixed annuity, nor are there any with a bank CD.[25] You know the bank is making money as they are using your money by lending it out, and the rate they give you is what you receive without a direct cost. The same thing is true with the insurance company. Although they don't lend out your money, they do earn interest on your money which allows them to give you a fixed guaranteed rate for the term of the contract.

Honestly, I like fixed annuities; they are simple and easy to understand. However, we need higher interest rates to make them more attractive. If interest rates do go up, we can look at a laddered fixed annuity strategy to generate the Retirement Paycheck. We have to allow for flexibility in one's plan as things will change over time, and what worked yesterday will be very different tomorrow. In my years of being a financial advisor, I have not been able to use fixed annuity or bank CD strategies due to interest rates. Although we would have been able to use these strategies back in the 1980s as interest rates were much higher back then, but, so was your mortgage rate!

Fixed Index Annuity

The fourth type of annuity is the fixed index annuity. The popularity of fixed index annuities has truly exploded over the last 15 years due to the low-interest rate

---

[25] https://www.newyorklife.com/articles/cd-vs-fixed-deferred-annuity#:~:text=Earnings%20on%20CDs%20are%20taxable,tax%20deferral%20may%20be%20helpful.

environment. The fixed index annuity allows one to invest money without market risk. The annuity is fixed, which means your principal is guaranteed against loss. However, the interest you earn is not known as it is attached to the performance of an index, meaning that your money isn't invested in the index, but the interest you earn is based on that index. To keep it simple, let's say we buy a ten-year contract, and the index of choice is the S&P 500. A fixed index annuity generally has a cap on earnings or a participation rate.[26] If the cap is 5%, that is the maximum interest you can earn over the crediting term. In most cases, the crediting term is 1 year. If your anniversary date is January 1st, then you can earn a total of 5% over the next year closing on December 31st. If the S&P goes up 4%, you make 4%, if it goes up 5%, then you make 5%, and if it goes up 6%, then you make 5%. You see, you can't make any more than the stated cap rate.

The participation rate strategy is similar, so let's say the participation rate is 50%. This means that you will earn half of what the S&P 500 earns every year. If the S&P is up 5%, then you make 2.5%, if the S&P is up 10%, then you make 5%, and if the S&P is up 20%, then you make 10%. As you can see, there are advantages and disadvantages to the

---

[26] https://www.forbes.com/advisor/retirement/fixed-index-annuity/

participation rate strategy over the strategy with a cap.[27] You can potentially earn more in the participation rate strategy, but in order for that to happen, the S&P, using 50% as the participation rate, would have to earn greater than 10% in return over a given year. Otherwise, you would be better off in the 5% cap strategy. As of writing this, current caps had increased up to 7.5% on the S&P 500.

There are quite a few different crediting strategies for a fixed index annuity, but I think you understand the basic concept. Now, the reason these products are so popular is that you can't lose money, and your gain is locked in on your anniversary date every year. There are benefits to this, and I do like this strategy when it comes to having a safety bucket with some of your retirement savings. However, there are many different varieties of fixed index annuities, as some lock in the gain every year (my preference), every 2 years, and every 3 years. In my opinion, if you are to put money into a fixed index annuity that locks in the gain every 2 or 3 years versus the 1 year, then those products had better outperform the 1-year lock-in. For most of my clients, the products that locked in the gain every year, using the S&P 500 as the index, outperformed those that locked in the gain every 2 or 3 years. Moreover, many of the strategies in a product that locks in every 2 or 3 years are based on volatility-controlled indexes. The reason

---

27 https://www.annuity.org/annuities/types/indexed/participation-rate/

volatility-controlled indexes became popular with fixed index annuities is that interest rates were so low that, for a while, we couldn't get very good caps or participation rates using the S&P 500 index. So, these volatility-controlled index choices come out offering 150% participation with your gain locked in every 3 years.[28] I must admit, I once fell victim to this marketing. It has not been all bad depending on when you started, but again, my clients using the S&P 500 as the index of choice, and locking in the gain every year, have outperformed all of my clients using other fixed index annuities that locked in the gain every 2 or 3 years. Now, I am not against volatility-controlled indexes, but I do prefer the gain to be locked in every single year. Diversification is key, so there is a benefit to using other index strategies, especially when markets become volatile. My advisors do use fixed index annuities in our planning for our clients, and I like to use these products as a way to replace longer-duration bond funds. As already mentioned, bond funds are subject to interest rate risk,[29] whereas the fixed index annuity is not. Most of the fixed index annuities I have offered my clients over the last five years have outperformed the typical bond funds I see in most people's portfolios. Something worth noting is that the S&P strategy, within all fixed index annuities, doesn't offer you dividends. You are not actually invested in the

---

[28] https://www.clickquotesave.com/volatility-controlled-index-strategies/

[29] https://www.investopedia.com/terms/i/interestraterisk.asp

S&P 500, so you don't receive those dividends and only receive the price change of the S&P 500 over the crediting term. Let's look at an example of a withdrawal strategy using a 50% participation rate versus just investing in the S&P 500 using a 4% withdrawal rate.

It is the same example that I have previously used, but let me give you a reminder. Suppose we invest $1 million into the S&P 500 with dividends. In that case, we take out 4% per year for income and increase the income needed by 2% each year to account for inflation. We also show the 1% management fee included for those who currently pay a financial advisor. Also, we start the S&P returns at the worst possible time, January 1st of 2000. Again, we do this because your Retirement Paycheck needs to withstand the worst case.

GROWTH BUCKET	S&P 500	Net Growth	Income	Account Balance
2000	-9.10%	-10.10%	$40,000	$859,000.00
2001	-11.89%	-12.89%	$40,800	$707,474.90
2002	-22.10%	-23.10%	$41,616	$502,432.20
2003	28.68%	27.68%	$42,448	$599,057.11
2004	10.88%	9.88%	$43,297	$614,946.67
2005	4.91%	3.91%	$44,163	$594,827.85
2006	15.79%	14.79%	$45,046	$637,756.39
2007	5.49%	4.49%	$45,947	$620,444.23
2008	-37.00%	-38.00%	$46,866	$337,809.05
2009	26.46%	25.46%	$47,804	$376,011.53
2010	15.06%	14.06%	$48,760	$380,118.97
2011	2.11%	1.11%	$49,735	$334,603.32
2012	16.00%	15.00%	$50,730	$334,064.14
2013	32.39%	31.39%	$51,744	$387,182.61
2014	13.69%	12.69%	$52,779	$383,536.94
2015	1.38%	0.38%	$53,835	$331,159.64
2016	11.96%	10.96%	$54,911	$312,543.31
2017	21.83%	20.83%	$56,010	$321,636.43
2018	-4.38%	-5.38%	$57,130	$247,202.54
2019	31.49%	30.49%	$58,272	$264,302.14
2020	18.40%	17.40%	$59,438	$250,852.82
2021	28.71%	27.71%	$60,627	$259,737.48
Total Income			$1,091,959	

Figure 8

We start with $1 Million, and by the end of the first year, after you take out the $40,000 for income, you are left with $859,000. By the end of 2021, you are left with $259,737.

Now, suppose we use the same example with a fixed index annuity with a 50% participation rate. In that case, you will notice the S&P 500 returns are a little different, as I can't include the dividends when using a fixed index annuity strategy. We will take out the same 4%/year in withdrawals and increase by 2% for inflation. There is no management fee with a fixed index annuity, as the agents receive a commission.

Without S&P Dividends				
SAFE BUCKET	**S&P 500**	**Net Growth**	**Income**	**Account Balance**
2000	-10.14%	0.00%	$40,000	$960,000
2001	-13.04%	0.00%	$40,800	$919,200
2002	-23.37%	0.00%	$41,616	$877,584
2003	26.38%	13.19%	$42,448	$950,889
2004	8.99%	4.50%	$43,297	$950,334
2005	3.00%	1.50%	$44,163	$920,426
2006	13.62%	6.81%	$45,046	$938,060
2007	3.53%	1.77%	$45,947	$908,670
2008	-38.49%	0.00%	$46,866	$861,803
2009	23.45%	11.73%	$47,804	$915,046
2010	12.78%	6.39%	$48,760	$924,758
2011	0.00%	0.00%	$49,735	$875,023
2012	13.41%	6.71%	$50,730	$882,964
2013	29.60%	14.80%	$51,744	$961,898
2014	11.39%	5.70%	$52,779	$963,899
2015	-0.73%	0.00%	$53,835	$910,064
2016	9.54%	4.77%	$54,911	$898,563
2017	19.42%	9.71%	$56,010	$929,803
2018	-6.24%	0.00%	$57,130	$872,674
2019	28.88%	14.44%	$58,272	$940,415
2020	16.26%	8.13%	$59,438	$957,433
2021	26.89%	13.45%	$60,627	$1,025,533
Total Income Received			$1,091,959	

Figure 9

Wow, what a difference not losing money has on your retirement! You didn't earn as much in the up years of the S&P 500, but you also didn't take the losses in the down years. You can see the total income received in both scenarios is exactly the same. Risk has a powerful impact on your retirement income strategy. In the above example eliminating the risk allowed for the 4% withdrawal strategy to work. In the years the S&P 500 was negative, you received no interest credit. This means you took out the principal to cover the income need; however, you pretty much maintained your money throughout the illustration. The lowest your money dropped to was $861,803 in 2008. This is not a perfect strategy, but it is better than the alternative in the first illustration.

Lastly, the fixed index annuity offers a guaranteed income component just like the variable annuity. Many times, there will be a bonus involved which offers the client "free money" to put with that insurance company.

Oftentimes, I hear people come in and say they went to a dinner seminar, and the speaker was pitching an annuity with a 25% bonus. They ask me, "Stephen, why would I not buy a product that gives me a 25% bonus?" and the honest answer is that you need to understand which side that bonus is on. Many times, that bonus is on the income rider side, which is a fictitious value, as that doesn't represent your real dollars invested. However, if you are purchasing a fixed index annuity for guaranteed income, then you do want to go out and get the highest bonus you can receive. This helps increase the income account value, which, in turn, leads to you getting a larger monthly paycheck. I am not against a bonus, but you need to understand how they work. Generally, if the insurance company is enticing you with a bonus, then they are also taking something away on the back end. Usually, the caps and participation rates are lower, which means your account value won't earn as much as it could have without the bonus. When the insurance company offers a bonus, and in many cases, that's just their way of marketing to get more premium into their products, it allows the salesperson to go out and entice you with "free money." Just know, there is no such thing as "free money." You do pay for that bonus in some way, as the pricing is built into the product. Most fixed index annuities don't have direct expenses, which is very different from their competitor, the variable annuity. However, that doesn't mean there isn't a cost, as the income rider for a fixed index annuity does have a direct cost. It's just that some insurance companies have found a way to build that direct cost into the product, so the client doesn't see that there is one. Again, it all comes down to the marketing of these products, and insurance companies have become very clever in their marketing.

I am not against a fixed index annuity that provides a pension payment in retirement as long as you know what you are giving up. Some people feel more comfortable with having a known paycheck every single month, but it does come at a cost that is different in every annuity, depending on the product. (If you want to learn more about fixed index annuities, email me at info@swp360.com. The world of annuities is constantly evolving, and we are always looking at annuity strategies to help our clients protect their retirement savings and generate income.)

One last point on fixed index annuities; I mentioned cost, and that cost can come in many different ways. There could be a direct fee or a spread charge. You could end up giving up your account value over time due to low caps and/or participation rates once you turn on the income rider. The other thing you need to know is those caps and participation rates can be adjusted by the insurance company on your anniversary.[30] I have seen my clients start with a participation rate of 54% in the S&P, and three years later, the participation rate is now 30%. You need to understand the moving parts in these products, as it does matter. I just want to be very clear about fixed index annuities; I LIKE THEM! However, I am very upfront about the costs and give importance to reading the fine print.

---

[30] http://theasagroup.com/wp-content/uploads/How-Caps-and-Par-Rates-are-determined.pdf

Income Rider

Let's dive into the details on the income rider. The income rider is how the annuity provides guaranteed income payments without annuitizing the annuity.[31] When you annuitize, you give up the money you put in for a guaranteed paycheck. I have a client that inherited an annuity from her father, who had already decided how his three daughters would take the distributions from the annuity. He selected the lifetime payout with a 30-year period certain. The value for each child was about $750,000, and they will receive $2,500/month or $30,000/year. If you multiply that over 30 years, they will receive $900,000 in payments. Now, think about that as $750,000 turning into $900,000 over 30 years. Does that sound like a good investment choice? It would be a good investment if you still had the $750,000 at the end of the 30 years, but you don't. My client and her sisters will have nothing left to pass on to their children, as that is what annuitization does. Just so you know the numbers, the compounded rate of return over 30 years is 0.61%/year. We can do better than that in a bank CD today.

The income rider does somewhat solve this problem, as you are not annuitizing. Below is an example of how the income rider works. You can see there are two sides to the annuity, the account value and the income value. We are

---

[31] https://myannuityguy.com/income-riders/

going to apply a 10% bonus to the income value, as this is typical when purchasing an annuity with an income rider. We are also using a 7% roll-up rate on the income value, again very typical, and will assume no growth in the account value. This is not likely, as you will get some growth, but I am just trying to illustrate the point of the income rider.

Amount Invested	$500,000		
Rollup Rate	7%		
Bonus	10%		
		Account Value	**Income Value**
	Start	$500,000	$550,000
	After Year 1	$500,000	$588,500
	After Year 2	$500,000	$629,695
	After Year 3	$500,000	$673,774
	After Year 4	$500,000	$720,938
	After Year 5	$500,000	$771,403
	After Year 6	$500,000	$825,402
	After Year 7	$500,000	$883,180
	After Year 8	$500,000	$945,002
	After Year 9	$500,000	$1,011,153
	After Year 10	$500,000	$1,081,933

Figure 10

The 'Income Value' rolls up at a compounded 7% rate for a total value at the end of 10 years of $1,081,933. What you have to know is that it is not your money. This is just the number the insurance company will use to determine the paycheck you will receive for life. Had you purchased this annuity at age 55 and planned to take income at age 65, your income from the annuity could be $48,686/year for a joint payment (covers both married people) or $59,506 on a single life payout. I am using a 4.5% rate on the joint payout and 5.5% on the single-life payout. Every insurance company has different rates, but the rates I am using are close enough for the illustration.

I assumed no growth on the account value side. You can see the $500,000 invested is still $500,000 at the end of 10 years. This is not likely to happen, but this is how the income rider is sold. The income rider is insurance against the worst-case scenarios. Your money not earning any interest over ten years would be the worst case in a fixed index annuity. In order for this to happen, the S&P 500 would have to be negative ten years in a row. I am not saying it can't happen, but that it is unlikely to happen. Let's use the joint-life payout of $48,687/year, as that would be a 9.7% payout off of the account value ($48,687/$500,000). The point I am trying to make is that you are going to spend down the $500,000 that you invested. The account value in this example will go to zero over time. If we continue to assume no growth on the $500,000, the illustration below will show you how long the money will last.

	Income Received	Ending Account Value
After Year 11	$48,687	$451,313
After Year 12	$48,687	$402,626
After Year 13	$48,687	$353,939
After year 14	$48,687	$305,252
After Year 15	$48,687	$256,565
After year 16	$48,687	$207,878
After Year 17	$48,687	$159,191
After Year 18	$48,687	$110,504
After year 19	$48,687	$61,817
After year 20	$48,687	$13,130
Total Income Received	$486,870	

Figure 11

After 20 years, assuming the worst-case scenario, where the contract earns 0% interest on the account value each year, you still don't have your original $500,000 investment back. You can see, at the end of year 20, the account value is almost exhausted. Once the account value is exhausted, the paycheck of $48,687 does continue to get paid, as that is why you purchased the income rider in the first place. It's basically insurance against running out of money. Let's say we continued the illustration through 30 years; the total amount of income received would now be $973,740. The contract was purchased at age 55, and now 30 years later, the client is 85 years of age, so over a 30-year time period, the $500,000 investment turned into $973,740, which is a 2.25% compounded rate of return, and you have nothing left to leave to your heirs. The income rider didn't give up the money immediately, which is what an immediate annuity would do, but over time, the account value did hit zero. I must admit, while I do understand the concept of insuring your retirement with income, I don't like these numbers. You are giving up your money to receive a guaranteed paycheck. If you want to protect yourself from doom and gloom scenarios, then the income rider is for you. But I don't believe in doom and gloom scenarios, and I hate the idea of giving up my money[31]

I will discuss a quick example assuming that the account value had not earned zero interest. Let's now assume a 4% average on the account value, we are still taking the income starting at the end of year 10, and the income is still $48,687. Earning interest on the account value didn't change the income payout, as the income rider value is still higher than the account value.

Amount Invested	$500,000
Rollup Rate	7%
Bonus	10%
Interest Earned	4%

	Account Value	**Income Value**
Start	$500,000	$550,000
After Year 1	$520,000	$588,500
After Year 2	$540,800	$629,695
After Year 3	$562,432	$673,774
After Year 4	$584,929	$720,938
After Year 5	$608,326	$771,403
After Year 6	$632,660	$825,402
After Year 7	$657,966	$883,180
After Year 8	$684,285	$945,002
After Year 9	$711,656	$1,011,153
After Year 10	$740,122	$1,081,933

Figure 12

You can see the account value at the end of 10 years is now $740,122. The income account value is exactly the same as it was when the account value earned nothing. The income account value is still rolling up at 7% compounded each year. Now when we start taking the income out after year 10, this is what it now looks like.

	Income Received	**Ending Account Value**
After Year 11	$48,687	$721,040
After Year 12	$48,687	$701,195
After Year 13	$48,687	$680,555
After year 14	$48,687	$659,091
After Year 15	$48,687	$636,767
After year 16	$48,687	$613,551
After Year 17	$48,687	$589,406
After Year 18	$48,687	$564,295
After year 19	$48,687	$538,180
After year 20	$48,687	$511,020
Total Income Received	$486,870	

Figure 13

After 20 years, this doesn't look so bad anymore. The $500,000 investment paid out $48,687 each year, totaling $486,687, and you still have $511,020 left. If you passed away at the end of year 20, your beneficiaries would receive $511,020. This means your $500,000 investment turned into $997,890 (The $486,687 you received in payments plus the $511,020 remaining account value). That is a 3.52% compounded rate of return over 20 years. See below for how the numbers look after 30 years.

	Income Received	Ending Account Value
After Year 21	$48,687	$482,774
After Year 22	$48,687	$453,398
After Year 23	$48,687	$422,847
After Year 24	$48,687	$391,074
After Year 25	$48,687	$358,030
After Year 26	$48,687	$323,664
After Year 27	$48,687	$287,924
After Year 28	$48,687	$250,754
After Year 29	$48,687	$212,097
After Year 30	$48,687	$171,894
Total Income Received	$973,740	

Figure 14

The math after 30 years is that your $500,000 investment turned into $973,740 in payments, and your death benefit is now $171,894. If you take the $973,740 in payments plus the remaining account value of $171,894, that would equal a total benefit of $1,145,634 for a 2.8% compounded rate of return over the life of the contract.

I believe that this is not the best use of one's money. However, if the client feels more secure having a reliable paycheck in retirement, then I am ok with it. You now know how the income rider works and that the cost, in the end, is your money.

Quick note; there are Fixed Index Annuity contracts offering inflation protection on the income.[32] You will run out of money on the account value side faster, and the illustration shown to you will most likely not come true. They also adjust the payout factor on the income value. So, rather than receiving 4.5% for a married couple, you might start at 3.75% since the income will increase over time. Again, you need to understand the questions to ask when looking at products like this.

I hope this chapter has provided you with a lot of information as it relates to generating a Retirement Paycheck. There is no right or wrong way to do it as long as you understand the pros, cons, and costs. Diversification is very important when building the Retirement Paycheck. Nothing is perfect, and nothing will ever be perfect. Markets and interest rates are always fluctuating, and your retirement income plan needs to evolve as things change. If you were to retire today, your Retirement Paycheck could look very different three years from now, depending on what interest rates do. The Retirement Paycheck plan needs to be managed, updated, and constantly reviewed. This is where a financial advisor can help you. Later in this book, I will set the proper expectations for hiring the right financial advisor. Meanwhile, if you have questions about

---

[32] https://www.annuityexpertadvice.com/inflation-protected-annuity/

building the Retirement Paycheck, we are here to help. Send me an email at info@swp360.com for any assistance.

Important Information from Chapter 2:

1. Dividends are a great way to generate the Retirement Paycheck in up and down markets. If the portfolio is diversified and managed well, the dividends will remain even when markets don't perform well.
2. Annuities have pros and cons, so make sure you read the fine print. Annuities are not bad, but you need to understand the moving parts.

Chapter 3: Taxes

Building a Tax-efficient Retirement Paycheck

Taxes are a very important part of building the Retirement Paycheck as it's not about how much you make but how much you can spend. Taxes will erode your purchasing power over time, and you need to have a plan to minimize the impact of taxation on your Retirement Paycheck. Remember the three-legged stool from the first chapter, that is, social security, pension, and savings, which make up your Retirement Paycheck? This chapter will focus on helping you manage the taxes on two of the three legs as, in most cases, we can't help to minimize the impact of taxes on a pension (unless a lump-sum distribution to a rollover IRA is an option).

Let's start with your savings, and more specifically, tax-deferred IRA and 401k accounts. For most people, the largest paycheck of their life is when they retire and roll over their 401k balance into their IRA.[33] There are many benefits to doing this, and I will touch on the rollover process a little later in this book. Most people tax-defer their 401k accounts, which means they don't pay any taxes on their money,

---

[33]https://www.investopedia.com/articles/personal-finance/071715/8-reasons-roll-over-your-401k-ira.asp

receive a tax deduction for the contribution throughout their working years, and watch it grow into their retirement nest egg that is now 100% TAXABLE!

Believe it or not, they did everything right! The thought process behind the tax deferral was that they would have a lower income in retirement compared to when they were working for 40 years. In some cases, this is true, but for many, I find that they make just about the same money in retirement as well, which keeps them in the same income tax bracket. However, if we go back 40 years, when they would have started their career, tax brackets were very different from what they are today. None of us knew that tax brackets would be lower than where they were when we first started working, and the thought process behind the tax deferral couldn't have predicted where income tax brackets were going over our careers. But the good news is that income tax brackets have come down, and that tax deferral strategy worked.

What you have to remember is that you basically made a deal with the federal government to pay them now or pay them later. With tax deferral, you chose later, and now every dollar in that 401k or IRA will be taxed at ordinary income rates, albeit at a lower tax bracket than they were when you started working. How many of you think income tax rates will go lower over time? I have never had anyone answer "yes" to that question, as most Americans believe that the tax rates will go up over time to account for the many challenges the US economy is currently facing. Some of those challenges include the ballooning national debt, the solvency of programs like social security and Medicare, and the fact that the working population is getting smaller with baby boomers retiring.

You have not just been compounding your money but also "their" money. Remember from chapter one, it's theirs, spelled THE IRS! You know that every dollar you take out of that rollover IRA account will be taxed at ordinary income rates. If you feel tax rates are going higher over time, then you should consider a plan that includes paying the taxes at today's lower rates.

Can someone tell me what the 1997 taxpayer relief act gave us?

Answer: **ROTH IRA**

The ROTH IRA is the most powerful and the most underutilized retirement account option we have in the United States.[34] ROTH IRA accounts became available in 1998 and were named after Delawares Senator; William ROTH, just in case you were wondering.

From this point on, we will focus on this ROTH IRA vehicle. Let's start with the basics of contributing money to a ROTH IRA and how it works. If you are under the age of

---

34 https://www.forbes.com/advisor/retirement/roth-ira-benefits/

50, you can contribute up to $6,000 of after-tax money to a ROTH IRA. Now, the after-tax contribution is important to understand because you don't receive a tax deduction on that contribution. You do receive a tax deduction if you contribute to a regular tax-deferred IRA, which also has a $6,000 limit. But if you are over the age of 50, you get a $1,000 per year catch-up contribution, making the maximum contribution in 2022 $7,000/year.[35]

Before we move further, let's make sure we understand what a tax deduction is. If you make $100,000/year in income and contribute to a regular tax-deferred IRA ($6,000), then your taxable income for that year would be $94,000, as you deferred the taxes on the $6,000 contribution to the IRA. The same would be true with a tax-deferred 401k, as the money you contribute is deferred, which lowers your overall taxable income. There is nothing wrong with this strategy as it helps manage your taxes in your working years by allowing you to invest money tax-deferred and take a deduction, thereby lowering your overall taxable income so your income is most likely higher than it would be when you retire.

ROTH IRA and ROTH 401k accounts don't receive a tax deduction as you have already paid the taxes on those contributions. However, the interest you earn will be 100% TAX-FREE for the rest of your life. The question is, do you

---

35 https://www.schwab.com/ira/roth-ira/contribution-limits

want to pay the taxes on the seed or the harvest? Let me see if I can make this picture clearer for you. Now, keep in mind the ROTH IRA wasn't available back in the 1980s, but my example will still make the point. If you had put $6,000/year (you couldn't do this back then) into a ROTH IRA every year for 40 years, and starting in 1981 through 2021, invested in the S&P 500, which averaged 11.8%/year over that time period, you would have tax-free $4.8 million in that account. Over this time period, you contributed $240,000 of your own money after tax, and it grew to $4.8 million. The seed is the $240,000 that you contributed, while the harvest is the $4.8 million it grew into. You paid the tax on the seed and now owe nothing on the harvest. Had you done the exact same thing with a traditional tax-deferred IRA, you would have the same $4.8 million, but it would all be taxable at ordinary income rates. With the ROTH IRA, you paid taxes on $240,000, or $6,000 per year, as that was the amount of money you contributed. The taxes on $6,000/year are a small price to pay, given that it grew to $4.8 million over 40 years. Do you want to pay taxes slowly over time on a total of $240,000, or do you want to pay the taxes on the $4.8 million? I think you now have a better understanding of the power of the ROTH IRA.

Without knowing your financial situation, I can't tell you to use a ROTH or a regular IRA. The same thing would be true with a ROTH 401k and a regular 401k. In many cases, I have people contribute to the tax-deferred 401k and make contributions to their ROTH IRA. Yes, you can do both depending on your income. In 2022, if you are single and making more than $144,000/year, you will not be able to contribute to a ROTH IRA. Similarly, if you are married and making more than $214,000, you will not be able to contribute to a ROTH IRA. The amount you contribute can also vary with income as, if you are single and making under $129,000, you can contribute the full $6,000 to your ROTH (under age 50) with a $1,000 catch-up contribution for those over the age of 50 (So $7,000 limit). The same applies if you are married and making under $204,000. But if you are in between the above thresholds, then you can't contribute the maximum amount (talk to your accountant if you are in this situation).[35]

Now, 401k contributions work very differently as there are no income limitations to contributing to a 401k. This is why it would be important to know your financial situation as it relates to guiding you between a tax-deferred 401k and a ROTH 401k. Again, there is no right or wrong, as we just need to know where you are at today versus where you might be tomorrow. Retirement tax planning changes depending on the client's situation, legislative decisions, and where they will be once you retire. Many of my clients move states in retirement, which also needs to be considered when providing retirement tax planning.[36]

---

36 https://www.investopedia.com/ask/answers/100314/whats-difference-between-401k-and-roth-ira.asp

ROTH Conversions

The main focus of this chapter will be on the ROTH conversion. There is no limit to the amount of money you can convert from your tax-deferred 401k's and IRAs into a ROTH IRA, But the catch is, you have to pay the taxes on the conversion. I wouldn't really consider this to be a catch, as you owe the money, and every dollar you take out of those tax-deferred accounts is taxed at ordinary income rates. Again, you will have to decide whether to pay the government now or pay them later, but you will have to pay them. Many people get a little confused with the ROTH conversion as they feel they just lose money by paying the taxes. But I will explain this so that you understand the value a ROTH conversion can bring to your retirement. If you do this properly, it would not be a cost, and you would not be giving up any of your money. What you will give up is compounding the government's money.

Moving forward, a couple of topics that we are going to discuss in detail, since they relate to the ROTH conversion, are the break-even analysis and the loss of compounding of your money when you pay the taxes. Both of these are incorrect, and I will walk you through the reason why there is no break-even analysis and how you didn't give up compounding.

Take a look at the chart below (Figure 15); the IRA value is $100k, and if we do a conversion using a 22% tax bracket, you are left with $78,000. Now, it is better if you pay the taxes out of a cash account as that way, you maintain the $100k in the ROTH IRA. However, if you don't have the cash to pay the taxes, I want you to see that you are not hurting yourself by withholding the taxes from the IRA. Many people feel that once the taxes have been paid and you are left with $78,000, they need to "make that money back!" What I want you to understand is that the example below of $78,000 in the ROTH versus $100,000 in the IRA is perfectly EQUAL as long as we know you will be in a 22% tax bracket. The key is understanding the tax bracket you are in right now while working versus the bracket you might be in when you retire. I will help you understand how we build this.

If you have $100k in the IRA, knowing that you are in a 22% tax bracket, then you have to realize that every dollar you take out of the IRA is taxed at 22%. Meaning, you only have $78,000 that is actually spendable. By doing this conversion and withholding the taxes, the $78,000 in the ROTH is equal to the $100,000 in the IRA.

I have added 10% interest to both sides of this chart to paint a clear picture. Let's start with the $100k in the IRA earning 10%, which means you now have $110,000, as illustrated in the chart below. You need money, so you take a 5% withdrawal from the IRA, which would equal $5,500. You can't actually receive $5,500 as you have to pay the taxes. If we know you are in the 22% tax bracket, we need to withhold the taxes leaving you with $4,290. That $4,290 is the money you will receive, as that is the net result after paying the taxes.

Now, look at the ROTH IRA on the right side. We added 10% interest to the $78,000, which is exactly what we did with the IRA. After the 10% interest, you now have $85,800, and after you take out the same 5% withdrawal, you have $4,290. It is exactly the same as the IRA with $100,000. What this means is that you don't have a break-even analysis, and you don't need to get the $78,000 back to $100,000 as they are already equal (yes, you want your money to grow, but I think you understand my point). Secondly, you didn't give up any interest by paying the $22,000 in taxes, as you have the same $4,290 on both sides.

	IRA	Taxes/Benefits	ROTH IRA
	$100,000	22% (Tax Bracket)	$78,000
Interest	10%	$22,000 paid in taxes	10%
	$110,000		$85,800
Withdrawl	5%		5%
	$5,500		$4,290
	22%		
	$4,290		

Figure 15

Some of you might be thinking, if both of them are equal, why should we consider doing a ROTH conversion? So let's talk about the benefits of doing this conversion;

1. RMDs (Required Minimum Distributions): At the age of 72, you are required to take a distribution from your IRA and 401ks (unless you are still working for the company where your 401k is held) and pay the taxes.[37] The government has let you tax defer this money, and now it's time to start paying them back. The RMD will get larger over time as the government wants to collect more of the tax dollars that they are owed. By doing the ROTH conversion, you have already given the government the portion you owed them, and you don't have to take an RMD out of a ROTH IRA. The money can sit in the ROTH IRA 100% tax-free for the rest of your life.

   It was the Secure Act that changed the RMD age from 70.5 to 72. It was also the Secure Act that changed how non-spousal beneficiaries inherit IRAs. Prior to the Secure Act, non-spousal beneficiaries could have stretched the IRA distributions over their life time, thereby managing the taxes.[38] Now, under the Secure Act, all monies have to be distributed from the IRA within 10 years. There is no stretch IRA option anymore, and this has

---

37 https://www.irs.gov/retirement-plans/plan-participant-employee/retirement-topics-required-minimum-distributions-rmds

38 https://www.kitces.com/blog/secure-act-age-72-required-minimum-distribution-rmd-age-70-1-2-qcd-2020/

changed the game as it relates to legacy planning. In my opinion, here is what the Secure Act did; the government knows the baby boomer population will all actuarially pass away over the next 20 – 30 years, and the United States will go through the largest wealth transfer we have ever seen as trillions of dollars will move from one generation to the next. The government has just figured out how to get their hands on those tax dollars that much faster by eliminating the stretch IRA. By having the money in a ROTH IRA, your non-spousal beneficiaries avoid the taxes. Yes, they still do have to distribute the money out of the ROTH within 10 years, but it's all tax-free.

2. Social Security taxes: Monies distributed from a ROTH IRA don't count toward taxing your social security benefits. When distributions are taken from a tax-deferred IRA, that income is countable, and for many, the reason a high percentage of their social security benefits become taxable. The formula to determine how much of your social security benefits become taxable is called the provisional income formula; 100% MAGI (Modified Adjusted Gross Income) + 100% of tax-exempt interest (usually Municipal Bonds) + 50% of social security benefits, which is equal to your provisional income. Once you know this number, you have to apply the two tests, depending on whether you are married or single. If you are married and making over $32,000/year in provisional income, up to 50% of

social security becomes taxable at ordinary income rates. Or if you are married and making over $44,000 of provisional income, then up to 85% of social security becomes taxable. On the other hand, if you are single and making over $25,000/year in provisional income, then up to 50% of social security is taxable, and if you're making over $34,000 in provisional income, then up to 85% is taxable.

If you truly want to minimize taxes on your social security benefits, a ROTH Conversion strategy could provide what you are looking for.[39] This will depend on a few other factors, such as pension income, dividend income from non-qualified accounts, rental property income, wages, etc. There is a lot that can play into this, but if most of the monies are in qualified accounts (401k's and IRA's), the ROTH conversion strategy could really help minimize the impact of taxation on social security benefits.

3. If married, DEATH: Death can impact the surviving spouses' taxes in a big way. Most married couples file their taxes jointly, and once a spouse passes away, the surviving spouse now files single. There is a big difference in tax brackets for married people versus single people. If married, the 22% tax bracket ranges from $83,551 up to $178,150. If single, the 22% bracket ranges from $41,776 up to $89,075. As

---

[39] https://www.cnbc.com/2022/03/08/considering-a-roth-ira-conversion-heres-how-to-reduce-the-tax-bite.html

you can see, there is a big difference in those ranges. What this means is that the surviving spouse now has all of the IRA monies and could end up paying higher taxes on that money due to filing taxes single versus married.[40] For married people, taking advantage of the married tax brackets can help the surviving spouse, as ROTH IRA distributions are not taxable, and we can minimize the impact of death on the retirement tax plan.

4. Increase in tax rates: Currently, tax rates have been reduced due to the Tax Cuts and Jobs Act, which is set to expire at the end of 2025. Going into 2026, we are set to go back to the 2017 tax brackets, and most likely, they will be adjusted for inflation. Now, this doesn't mean things can't change due to new legislation that may be introduced between now and then, but unfortunately, we can't build a retirement tax plan based on the unknown, so we need to build the plan to account for going back to 2017 tax brackets. In 2017, the 25% tax bracket for married individuals was $75,901, up to $153,100 of income. If single, the 25% tax bracket was $37,951 up to $91,900. Currently, the 22% bracket for married couples is $83,551 up to $178,150, and it is $41,776 up to $89,075 for single files. I think you can see my point now. Wouldn't you rather pay the taxes in today's 22% and 24% brackets versus tomorrow's

---

[40] https://www.wsj.com/articles/taxes-after-death-of-a-spouse-irs-11635462166#:~:text=Some%20call%20this%20%E2%80%9Cthe%20widow's,with%20about%2020%25%20less%20income.

25% and 28% brackets? If you feel tax rates will be going lower, then you might not want to consider a ROTH conversion. However, as previously discussed, most people feel that tax rates will go up (but it is still unknown how much).

5. Medicare: There are pros and cons with Medicare premiums when doing the ROTH conversion. I have many of my clients doing ROTH conversions and taking their income up to $340,000, which is the top of the married 24% tax bracket. By doing this, we could be increasing Medicare Part B premiums. Medicare Part B premiums are determined by your income, two years in arrears. Now, this is temporary pain while doing the conversion, and in many cases, the temporary pain is worth it. If you are single, making under $91,000 or married under $182,000, then your Medicare Part B premium is $170.10/month. If you are single and making between $91,000 and $114,000 or married and making between $182,000 and $228,000, your Medicare Part B is $238.10. If single and making between $114,000 and $142,000 or married and making between $228,000 and $284,000, then Medicare Part B is $340.20. Similarly, if single and making between $142,000 and $170,000 or married and making between $284,000 and $340,000, then Medicare Part B is $442.30. These numbers are all for 2022. Premiums continue to go up with income, and you can visit the Medicare website for more

information: *https://www.medicare.gov/your-medicare-costs/part-b-costs.*

The ROTH conversion can also help this situation depending on how much money is in 401k's and IRA's that will require an RMD at the age of 72. By doing the conversion, and potentially paying more for Medicare Part B, you could end up keeping your income in the lowest brackets for Medicare Part B in the long run. Think about death for married people; by doing the conversion to a ROTH, you are giving the surviving spouse a chance to stay under the income limit for a single person. This conversion can cause some temporary pain but could really help avoid increased Medicare Part B premiums in the long run. Everyone has a different situation, and this is why it's important to work with a financial advisor and tax professional that thinks long-term about your taxes. Not all tax professionals think like this, so you need to be careful from whom you receive advice. Also, be aware of the 3.8% Medicare surcharge when doing a ROTH conversion (Discuss it with a tax professional).

6. Beneficiaries: I will keep this one short as monies that are passed on to beneficiaries in a ROTH IRA are 100% TAX-FREE. It's that simple. The best gift to give to your children and grandchildren is a tax-free gift.

7. Last, ROTH IRAs earn TAX-FREE interest. Once you do the conversion, the interest earned for the rest of your life will NEVER be taxed again.[41] I think that's pretty cool!

One thing to watch out for would be the 5-year rule with a ROTH Conversion. When you do the conversion, you will have immediate access to the remaining principal in the ROTH, but the gain is subject to a 5-year holding period before it can be accessed. However, ROTH IRAs follow FIFO, First in, First out. The first in is the principal, which means that's also the first out. In the above example, when converting $100k into a ROTH and you have $78k left, as long as you don't exhaust the $78k within 5 years (that's the principal), then you won't have a problem with this rule. For most of my clients, we are generating dividends for their retirement and will not go beyond the principal within 5 years, thereby negating the 5-year rule. If you do go beyond the principal within the 5 years, then you are losing the tax-free benefits of the ROTH IRA. My simple advice is, don't do that!

I can go on and tell you so much more as it relates to retirement tax planning, but this book would then be way

---

[41] https://www.investopedia.com/ask/answers/091815/how-does-roth-ira-grow-over-time.asp#:~:text=Key%20Takeaways,can't%20make%20a%20contribution.

too long. A great source for you would be to read Ed Slott's book "The New Retirement Savings Time Bomb." There is a lot of great information about retirement tax planning in this book. I have read both of his books, and a lot of what I have discussed in here is in his books.

Life Insurance

Life Insurance is a great vehicle to use for retirement tax planning, but you need to understand the moving parts. First, life insurance death benefits are 100% tax-free but countable in the estate. Most people don't have a federal estate tax problem as the exemptions are very high today due to the Tax Cuts and Jobs Act ($12.06 Million per person). My state, Illinois, does have a state estate tax, and that exemption limit is a lot lower ($4 Million per person). The reason I bring this up is that a life insurance death benefit could cause an estate tax problem if it puts the overall estate over these exemption limits. The way you avoid that is with an Irrevocable Life Insurance Trust (ILIT), which moves the life insurance outside of your estate, making it not countable.

If you want to pass money on tax-free, then life insurance could be a useful tool. Many times, I have found that life insurance is used to generate tax-free income. Before you do that, make sure you understand how tax-free income out of a life insurance policy works. First off, it's not really tax-free; this is due to the fact that you are borrowing your own money out of the policy. Loans are not subject to income taxes which is how life insurance gets away with a so-called tax-free distribution.[42] You do pay interest on the money you take out, but life insurance allows that money to still earn interest even though it is no longer in the policy. So, to try and keep this explanation simple, you need to understand the earnings potential within the life insurance policy and the loan rate, not just today's loan rate, but the highest loan rate the insurance company can charge. If rates go up, you will want to know this as you don't want to be in a situation where the loan rate exceeds what you can earn in the policy. That would cause the policy to go backward, and you could now create a very large taxable situation. The policy has to remain in force to avoid the taxes on the gains. If the policy lapses, then every dollar above and beyond your premium is 100% taxable.

I met with a gentleman and his wife who had a lot of money tied up in life insurance policies. They had purchased these policies many years ago, back in the day when I was a teenager. So, when I reviewed their current policies, I discovered a huge problem. First, they purchased the original policies when the interest rate was 8% and the loan rate was 6%. Now, this works as the 8% earned is more than the 6% paid in interest. However, due to interest rates coming down, the earned rate was now 4%, and the loan rate had a floor of 6%, meaning it was still 6%. This

---

42 https://www.investopedia.com/ask/answers/102015/do-beneficiaries-pay-taxes-life-insurance.asp#:~:text=Generally%20speaking%2C%20when%20the%20beneficiary,to%20pay%20taxes%20on%20it.

killed their policies. The couple were in a situation where they would be taxed on almost $750,000 of monies that had been distributed to them from their life insurance policies, and they had no choice as the policies were going to lapse. There were many mistakes made in order to end up in this situation, as the advisor and/or insurance company should have warned them of this a long time ago. I don't know why that wasn't done, and now they owed a lot in taxes.

If I had to guess, there was a notification sent out informing the client that their policies would be under the over-loan protection agreement. Many life insurance policies have this feature, as it prevents the policy from lapsing. However, you won't be able to take any more money out, so relying on life insurance for retirement income when you don't understand the moving parts could backfire on you.

As a Fiduciary, I am not against anything, but my experience has shown that life insurance is not a great vehicle to use for retirement income. Today, they call it the LIRP, which is the Life Insurance Retirement Plan, and many people are out there selling the LIRP and trying to convince clients to put all of their hard-earned 401k and IRA monies into life insurance. This is similar to a ROTH conversion, where you pay the taxes and then put them into the life insurance after tax. The problem with this is there are a lot of moving parts. Many of the policies that I see are built with level death benefits. A level death benefit doesn't buy the client the highest death benefit, but it doesn't buy the lowest either. This means that there is a higher cost of insurance in the policy, which slows the growth of the cash value. If you are buying life insurance to provide tax-free income, you want the lowest death benefit you can get to get the lowest cost of insurance. The way you do this is with an increasing death benefit option, and once premiums are fully paid up, you drop the death benefit again, keeping the cost of insurance low. The goal is to grow the cash value, not the death benefit. In my opinion, the main reason that the level death benefit is sold over the increasing one is agent commissions. The higher the death benefit, the more the agent gets paid.

Let's look at some examples so we can paint a clearer picture. Consider a female aged 55, with a preferred health rating (underwriting is required), who will fund the LIRP strategy with $30,000/year for 10 years. The initial death benefit is $734,462 and will remain that way until distributions start as she reaches the age of 70. We want to give the policy 15 years to accumulate before taking loans. Starting at the age of 70, she can potentially withdraw $33,211/year until she reaches 90. I stopped the income at 90 (I could have shown it until age 100, but it would have been lesser).

Now, we take the same example, but instead of a level death benefit of $734,462, we will build the policy to start with a death benefit of $394,735. By year 10, the death benefit jumps up to $735,772; up till then, when all premiums would have been paid, we drop the death benefit, starting year 11, to $432,479. The income the client can potentially receive is $37,619, starting from age 70 until age 90. That is $4,408 more per year, or $92,568 more over the client's lifetime, just by building the policy correctly.

You probably noticed that the death benefit had been lowered in the second example. But that's what we want, as we are not trying to buy death benefits. The lower the death benefit, the more the cash value can grow due to lower costs. Moreover, the commission paid to the agent in the first example is $20,807, as this example had a higher death benefit. Whereas, the second example paid the agent $11,182.

I am not against agents getting paid, but these kinds of things need to be disclosed as there are a lot of moving parts within these policies. If income is the end goal, then the lower death benefit needs to be applied regardless of what the agent gets paid.

Another area of concern is that the insurance company reserves the right to change the caps and participation rates in index universal life policies. Very similar to the index annuity concept explained earlier, the IUL goes up with the index, locks in the gain, and doesn't participate in the downside of the index. However, the caps and participation rates can change every crediting term. I own a policy for my own life, and when I purchased it, the cap on the S&P was 13.5%. My policy was designed to average 6%, and this was conservative, as the top rate was 8%. Well, 7 years later, my cap is now 7.4%, and my policy, in a very strong S&P market between November of 2014 and November of 2021, has averaged 5%. My policy has no chance of matching the illustration, which means the income won't be as illustrated. I have a big problem with this, as retirement income needs to be known. With the LIRP strategy, the client will need to get an in-force illustration run every single year to determine the "safe" amount they can take out each year. The "safe" amount is important because you don't want to take out too much, causing the policy to lapse over time. LIRP illustrations show a consistent rate of return year over year. This isn't how it actually works, as you might have good years and some years where you earn nothing. If you are using the IUL, you can't lose money due to a market correction, but not making money can be very damaging to the LIRP strategy, especially in the years you start taking income.

The most important part of the LIRP strategy is understanding the 'loan.' Again, it's not tax-free because you are borrowing your own money out of the policy, and you will have to pay interest on that loan. Interest rates have been low since 2008, making these policies very attractive. But now that we are starting to see the rates increase, agents and clients need to be aware of how high the insurance company can raise the rates. My policy has a current loan rate of 4.25%. Now, it has earned 5%, meaning my earn rate is greater than my loan rate. However, the insurance company reserves the right to raise the loan rate as high as 6%. If that were to happen, I would have a problem with my policy as a loan rate higher than what the policy can earn will cause the policy to fail over time or force the over-loan protection agreement to be implemented.

Life insurance is a complicated tool; it can be beneficial, but you really need to understand the moving parts. The illustrations being built are not worth the paper they are printed on. Make sure you read the fine print and get an understanding of what the insurance companies can change throughout the policies' life. In my case, I will be moving my life insurance policy to a different insurance company that doesn't have a cap on earnings. I am younger, so I have time, and I want the highest potential earnings I can get as I have to make up for poor performance over the last 7 years, which is frustrating because the S&P 500 has averaged 12.46%/year (without dividends as IUL's don't give you S&P dividends) between December of 2014 through December of 2021 (my policy went in force at the end of November which is why I used December of 2014 through December of 2021).

We could talk a lot more about taxes in retirement. As a matter of fact, we could write 10 books on just that topic alone. However, if you read Ed Slott's book that I mentioned above, I think you will get most of what you need. Other topics that are important: Capital Gains taxes, taxes on dividends, rental income, depreciation recapture, NUA strategies for those that work for a publicly-traded company and have purchased that stock within their 401k, and more.

I can't recommend everyone to do a ROTH conversion as everyone's situation is different, and I need to understand what you have and what you are trying to accomplish. This happens within our planning process, and if you want to explore our planning process, you can give us a call or send me an email (info@swp360.com).

Important Information from Chapter 3:

1. Consider doing a ROTH Conversion, but you need to understand the tax bracket you are in today while working versus tomorrow, when you would be retired. Building the Retirement Paycheck will help you understand where your income comes from and how it is taxed.
2. The Retirement Paycheck needs to be reliable, and I don't feel Life Insurance policies can provide reliable retirement income. There are a lot of moving parts, and understanding how the loans work is very important to make the policy work.

Chapter 4: Let's Build a Plan!

The job of a financial advisor is to help the client put all the pieces together. When new prospects walk through my door after attending one of my live workshops, they don't have an idea of what they are looking for. We like to set proper expectations right from the beginning, starting with putting the 'pieces' together. So, let's walk through a typical example of what happens when someone first approaches me to seek financial services.

Whether you are single, married, divorced, or widowed, it doesn't matter since the goal of this chapter is to help you understand how we start putting the pieces together. I will start with how we start building the Retirement Paycheck for a typical client.

The first thing to understand about the client(s) is when their desired retirement date is. Now, there are two parts to this question:

1. When does the client want to retire?

2. When CAN the client retire?

Unfortunately, the answers to both these questions don't always match as we need to help the client understand what is realistic and possible. So, I start by gathering all of their financial information, which includes:

1. Dates of Birth
2. Social Security benefit amounts at full retirement age (PIA)
3. Home value and mortgage amount, as well as other real estate investments, if they have more
4. Current job salaries
5. Pension information if they have a pension (lump sum, single and joint payout options)
6. 401k values, as well as how much they are contributing and what the match is
7. IRA and ROTH IRA values
8. Brokerage account values, annuity values, and life insurance policy information
9. Healthcare plans, if they retire before Medicare
10. Estate plan (Do they have a Will and Trust in place)?
11. Do they have kids and grandkids?
12. Budget – This is the big one!

The budget includes the following three main types of expenses:

a. Basic living expenses: These would include property taxes, mortgage (if they still have one), food and dining out, utilities, insurances, gas, cell phone and internet bills, pet bills, home improvement costs, hair, clothing, and all other miscellaneous expenses.

b. Healthcare costs: I separate medical expenses from basic living expenses as healthcare inflates at a different rate.
c. Extras: I add the travel budget, new car budget, extra expenses, and other one-off expenses separately. Remember, retirement is not about how much money you have but how much you spend.

Once I have all of the above information, we use our planning software to build their plan. The planning software will guide my clients on when they can retire, when to take social security, and how budget changes impact their retirement plan. This way, I can apply inflation, tax, and market risk factors and show what an early death might do to the plan.

I also met people who were divorced but had remarried. They had a guaranteed pension from their job and took the single life payout on that pension due to the divorce. But now that they have remarried, this hurts the new spouse if the person with the pension passes away. We have to consider everything when building the Retirement Paycheck. Once the plan has been built, we can now make specific investment recommendations to accomplish the plan. This is how we build the Retirement Paycheck.

When I talk about investing money, I like to use a three-bucket approach:

1. Safety: I like having some safe money, which you know will always be there and isn't subject to market fluctuations.
2. Income: This bucket generates the income need using savings. We use the dividend approach to accomplish this goal.
3. Growth: The money in this bucket can take the long-term investment approach as we don't need it to provide for retirement income needs. This means that we can watch this bucket go down in value when the markets are not performing well and patiently wait for markets to recover. There is no need to panic since we don't need the money in this bucket for income.

Every client is different, with different requirements, as clients with larger pensions may not need as much money generating income. They can afford more risk as the pension covers their income need. Other clients need every dollar they have to generate a paycheck. There is no right or wrong, as it depends on the client's needs, but many people feel they shouldn't take as much risk as they age. I don't feel risk has anything to do with age and has everything to do with what the client can afford and what they are comfortable with. I have clients who don't need their money as their income need is covered by pension and social security, but they don't want to lose a single dollar in the stock market. While I have other clients in the same situation that want everything in the stock market. Hence, there is no right or wrong as long as the risk doesn't impact the Retirement Paycheck.

When building tax efficiencies into the plan, we must account for the current tax brackets, future tax brackets when the tax cuts and jobs act expires, and Medicare part B premiums. I use the charts below to explain how to do this.

2022 Tax Brackets:

2022 Federal Income Tax Brackets and Rates for Single Filers, Married Couples Filing Jointly, and Heads of Households

Tax Rate	For Single Filers	For Married Individuals Filing Joint Returns	For Heads of Households
10%	$0 to $10,275	$0 to $20,550	$0 to $14,650
12%	$10,275 to $41,775	$20,550 to $83,550	$14,650 to $55,900
22%	$41,775 to $89,075	$83,550 to $178,150	$55,900 to $89,050
24%	$89,075 to $170,050	$178,150 to $340,100	$89,050 to $170,050
32%	$170,050 to $215,950	$340,100 to $431,900	$170,050 to $215,950
35%	$215,950 to $539,900	$431,900 to $647,850	$215,950 to $539,900
37%	$539,900 or more	$647,850 or more	$539,900 or more

Source: Internal Revenue Service

Figure 16

2022 Medicare Part B Premiums:

If your yearly income in 2020 was			
File individual tax return	**File joint tax return**	**File married & separate tax return**	**You pay (in 2022)**
$91,000 or less	$182,000 or less	$91,000 or less	$170.10
above $91,000 up to $114,000	above $182,000 up to $228,000	not applicable	$238.10
above $114,000 up to $142,000	above $228,000 up to $284,000	not applicable	$340.20
above $142,000 up to $170,000	above $284,000 up to $340,000	not applicable	$442.30
above $170,000 and less than $500,000	above $340,000 and less than $750,000	above $91,000 and less than $409,000	$544.30
$500,000 or above	$750,000 or above	$409,000 or above	$578.30

Figure 17

Using the two charts above is how my team and I started building tax efficiencies. For example, if a client is currently working and is in the 22% tax bracket but will be in a 12% tax bracket when they retire, I can't suggest doing a ROTH conversion and paying 22% in taxes when they will only pay 12% when they retire.

I also can't suggest that every client either jump $91,000, if single, or $182,000, if married, in total income. By doing so, they would have increased Medicare Part B premiums. On top of that, the 3.8% surcharge on Medicare can also be added if we go above $200,000 (single) and $250,000 (married). These things need to be considered before doing the ROTH conversion. There are benefits to paying more temporarily, but that doesn't apply to everyone. Also, it should be noted that Medicare Part B premiums were based on your income two years ago. Notice the top of the chart says your yearly income in 2020.

I also look back at the 2017 tax brackets, as we are scheduled to go back after the Tax Cuts and Jobs Act expires at the end of 2025. RMDs need to be figured into these calculations as the RMD could cause the client to jump tax brackets. In this situation, I usually suggest we do the conversion, as the RMD will make it happen down the road anyways. By doing this, the money is in the ROTH IRA and not subject to an RMD or an increase in future tax rates.

Roth conversions are something we work on every year with our clients as things change from year to year. I have several clients that have 100% of their IRAs converted into a ROTH. We are generating all of their income in dividends out of the ROTH, and they are paying no income taxes on their social security due to the income coming out of the ROTH. The plan can work if you know how to put the pieces together.

When I design plans, I never like to tell a client they can or can't do something. My job is just to figure out how to make it happen; I can't always give clients what they want, but I do try my best.

As you can see, there is a lot to consider when putting all the pieces together and building each client's Retirement Paycheck. It can be more involved when adding life insurance and long-term care plans, as we need to pay for these things. The proper advisor can build this out for you and give you a real picture of what retirement will look like. Again, every advisor builds the Retirement Paycheck differently. As long as the paycheck is reliable, tax-efficient, and not subject to all of the ups and downs of the stock market, and if the sequence of return risk is understood, then there are many ways to do it, as I have illustrated in previous chapters. My firm, SWP, likes the dividend approach, and if you want to learn more about our dividend portfolios, you can email us (info@swp360.com).

There is not a lot to summarize in this chapter, as putting the pieces together will look different for everyone. In the next chapter, I will discuss how to hire the proper financial advisor and what things you should consider. Important information from chapter 4:

1. Build a plan and understand your budget needs. Once this is accomplished, we can build the Retirement Paycheck to match your needs.
2. The ROTH conversion will be different for everyone based on what they are trying to accomplish.
3. Don't forget about the 3.8% Medicare Surtax when doing ROTH Conversions.

Chapter 5: How to Find the Right Financial Advisor

As much as I would love everyone who reads this book to work with my firm, I know that's not plausible. So, I want to help you find the right advisor and set proper expectations. Not all financial advisors are the same, so it is extremely important to find the right advisor to help build your Retirement Paycheck. I often hear financial advisors tell their clients that they only manage money and don't get involved in retirement tax or estate planning. But I strongly believe that your advisor needs to do a lot more than just manage your money. They need to have knowledge about all areas important to your retirement plan.

I recently had a client call me who had moved to Pennsylvania. They lived in Illinois their whole lives and moved East to be closer to their kids. Since they needed to update their estate plan, they went to see an estate attorney. The estate attorney suggested they take their ROTH IRA out and put it in an irrevocable trust for Medicaid planning. When my client texted, asking me about moving the ROTH IRAs out of the estate, that meant they would no longer be in the ROTH. I immediately called them back while they were in a meeting with the attorney. I was on the phone with my clients, and as they sat in the estate attorney's office, I started asking the estate attorney questions that were related to his suggestion of moving the

ROTH IRA money out of the estate. He told me he wanted that money out of their estate to plan for the worst-case scenario of Medicaid planning.

Before I move further, I would like to explain what Medicaid planning is. When people don't have enough money to pay for long-term healthcare, they go to Medicaid for support. However, they generally have to go through Medicaid spend down if they have income and assets above the limits that qualify them for Medicaid.[43] You can't just go on Medicaid when you have $1 million in investable assets like my clients, who now live in Pennsylvania. I don't want to get too far into the weeds with this case, but because of their assets, this client would not have been able to qualify for Medicaid even if we moved the ROTH IRA money out of the estate. They still had another $1 million in IRA money that would make them ineligible for the aid. So, the attorney's suggestion to move the money out of the ROTH IRA and into an irrevocable trust didn't make any sense. It was just a sales pitch to get them to buy a trust they didn't need.

You can now see how these situations can be avoided when you work with a proper financial advisor that has knowledge about all related areas. You want to include your advisor in such decisions to ensure everything is set up correctly. The advisor will need the related documents as

---

[43] https://money.usnews.com/money/retirement/baby-boomers/articles/how-a-medicaid-spend-down-works

beneficiaries are supposed to be updated, and non-qualified accounts are changed to the trust names (if a trust is involved). The advisor should always know what's going on with the overall estate plan. Remember, the advisor doesn't draft the documents; that is the lawyer's job, but the advisor should be the one leading the way.

Taxes are a very interesting topic for most financial advisors. Many advisors don't want to be involved in tax planning as they tell their clients to speak with their accountants regarding them. I don't entirely agree with this strategy as the financial advisor needs to have strong tax knowledge to make important decisions for their client. When we deal with investments, we need to understand the impact of taxation on one's investments. Unfortunately, I see many non-qualified brokerage accounts come in that have a low-cost basis. I can't just sell off those positions to put a new investment plan in place. As financial advisors, we need to understand how to manage a client's tax situation when it comes to their investments. We also need to help the client build a tax-efficient Retirement Paycheck. So, if your financial advisor doesn't want to be involved in long-term retirement tax planning, I suggest you should start looking for a new advisor.

Another thing that these advisors do is throw around the word 'Fiduciary' a lot, so I want to make sure you understand what a Fiduciary is. A Fiduciary manages property or money on behalf of someone else, and the law requires them to manage the person's assets for their benefit, not their own. Every financial advisor will tell you that they are a fiduciary, for the most part, but I will be upfront and honest as I don't believe there is a single financial advisor that is truly a fiduciary. Why do I say that? Because we get paid to do our jobs. All of us want new clients as that grows our paychecks. Every advisor does the job differently, so it's up to you to determine what methodologies fit what you are looking for. Some advisors call themselves Fiduciary, but they push annuities onto you. At the same time, other advisors hate annuities and don't offer them to their clients at all. That is why it is very hard for anyone to truly call themselves "Fiduciary."

For me, being a Fiduciary means that the advisor offers all products without any bias. It means the advisors explain the pros, cons, and costs of all investment options and allow you to choose the right plan that makes the most sense for you. It means the advisor doesn't build anything up based on the products, nor do they tell you some investments are bad. The typical approach for people selling fixed index annuities is to scare you out of the stock market or entice you with a big bonus. This wouldn't be considered Fiduciary. The right advisor doesn't push anything on you or talk you out of anything as it's not their money, and it's not their decision how the money gets invested. A Fiduciary's job is to just explain the options you have, and then they leave it to you to make a decision. You shouldn't know how the advisor feels about annuities versus the stock market versus life insurance.

Obviously, as advisors, we all have opinions about the products; even I have made some of my opinions known in this book about the income riders on annuities and the life insurance retirement plan. What I hope I have done is made you aware of how these things work. There is a cost to everything, and my job is to make sure you understand these costs. There are not always "fees" as sometimes the cost is you giving up your money to the insurance company.

Working with a Fiduciary is important, but you need to understand what a fiduciary really is. Just because someone is a Certified Financial Planner (CFP) doesn't make them a fiduciary. Just because someone works for a big bank or an investment firm doesn't make them a fiduciary. Many of those firms are publicly traded, which means they report to shareholders, not clients. You need to make sure you understand the difference. But I consider myself a fiduciary, as well as every member of my team. Also, note that Significant Wealth Partners is a registered investment advisory firm, and we have a contractual responsibility to act as fiduciaries to our clients. I have trained my team not to have opinions regarding products but to review the pros, cons, and costs. We do get compensated for the work that we do, and we disclose that compensation to the client, as the client should know how we get paid.

A lot of advisors are "fee-only," meaning they charge you a fee to build your plan and give you recommendations on how to invest your money. They don't manage your money, which would typically earn a management fee, but they tell you how to invest your money. I will be upfront; I have never found even one of these plans to be good. The "fee-only" advisor advertises as a Fiduciary and then tells you to go buy the S&P 500 and total bond market ETFs. The "fee-only" advisor takes no responsibility for the success of your plan. They will often show you how the S&P and bond markets have averaged between 7 and 9% per year in total return and how you would be just fine. However, this year, more than any other year over the last 40 years, has proven that strategy to be wrong. Stock and bonds are both down, and the Fed will likely continue its rate hikes. Building the Retirement Paycheck based on what has happened in the past is a recipe for disaster.

Hiring the right financial advisor is a big decision, and finding the right firm that fits what you are looking for can be difficult. Usually, people don't know what they are looking for, so it helps to interview three or four firms to learn about the different strategies they employ. I strongly believe below are a few important things you need to look at before hiring a financial advisor:

1. Fees: I have gone back and forth on how much an advisor should charge for their services. If the advisor is holistic and can help in all areas of planning, then 1%/year is a good starting point. I don't believe you should be paying more than that.
2. Ensure the advisor has knowledge in all areas of financial planning (managing money, building the

Retirement Paycheck, taxes, estate planning, long-term care, Medicare, Social Security, Medicaid, and insurance planning).

3. Make sure the advisor has a website and an office listed on brokercheck.com, so you can look them up.
4. Make sure the custodian is a large firm like Charles Schwab, Fidelity, or E-trade. If you work with a big firm, then your money would be with a large custodian already (Merrill Lynch would be an example).
5. Check how many years of experience the advisor has. We all have to start somewhere and need people to take a chance on us while we are young in this business. However, ensure they have a good mentor in place that is helping them. Just because someone is young doesn't mean they are not capable. I was young once, and I am very thankful for the clients who gave me a chance. But let's flip that situation; if your advisor is over 60 years of age, it's high time to start interviewing other advisors.
6. The advisor should never push products or give you deadlines. Many insurance companies put marketing schemes together to push products, and they put cutoff dates on their offers. Don't fall for this approach.
7. Flexibility – The advisor has to build flexibility into your plan. We can't lock up all of your money based on today's tax laws, interest rates, etc. This is because we don't know what we don't know, and flexibility is very important when building your Retirement Paycheck.
8. Don't pay a financial advisor to buy you mutual funds and ETFs. Forgive me, but this is a cost to your overall

plan, as you can buy mutual funds and ETFs yourself. If you don't know how, then I would suggest you learn. The typical approach is you own a diversified portfolio of funds such as large-cap, mid-cap, small-cap, international, and bonds. Some of the funds are growth, some are value, some provide income, and some are alternatives like commodities or gold. Again, you don't need to pay an advisor to buy this for you. There is a benefit to paying an advisor to build a properly structured income portfolio, as that takes a lot of time and management by the advisor. But in my mind, paying an advisor for the typical 60/40 plan is a cost to your retirement.

These were just my thoughts based on the experience I gained while doing this job. However, there are a lot more things to consider when hiring your financial advisor.

Important information from Chapter 5:

1. Understand what you are paying for when hiring a financial advisor. If you are going to pay an advisor, make sure they can do all aspects of the job.
2. Working with a fiduciary is important; just make sure you understand what that word really means.
3. There is value in having someone manage your money. It just doesn't come in the form of buying mutual funds and ETFs, as you can do that yourself.

Chapter 6: Everything I Didn't Talk About!

The goal of this book was to help people transition from their work paycheck to their Retirement Paycheck. I want to make that paycheck as tax efficient as possible using today's laws. Things are constantly changing, as I just read that the required minimum distribution age might increase to 75. This has not gone through yet, but as you can see, we always have to adjust plans.

I wanted to share many more topics outside this book's scope but didn't share them as I wanted this to be a short, quick read. One such topic I didn't spend a lot of time on is 'Social Security,' which is one of the three legs of your Retirement Paycheck plan. I teach classes on Social Security strategies, and let me tell you, every scenario is different. There is no right or wrong answer when taking Social Security, as you need to see how this decision impacts the overall financial plan. That's what I tell my clients. I don't have an opinion about when you should take it. Some people believe they should take it at 62, and others at 70. When you lay out the Retirement Paycheck plan, with tax efficiencies included, you get to see how taking Social Security at different times impacts all of this.

I don't want this to be a book about Social Security strategies, as that can be a whole book on its own. However, if you have questions about Social Security strategies, please email me at info@swp360.com.

Medicare is another important topic, and there is a lot to discuss here as well. The tax strategy also plays a part in your Medicare Part B premium, and understanding how Medicare works and picking the right plan can't be overlooked. Whether you go with Medicare Advantage or a Medigap plan depends on your situation, and having the right team walk you through your choices will help you make the right decision. I can't just tell you to buy Medigap plan G instead of plan N; everyone's situation is different, and everyone needs a different plan.

Charitable contributions can be a great way to minimize the tax impact on a ROTH Conversion. If you like giving money to charities, then you will want to familiarize yourself with the following three strategies:

1. Donor Advised Funds

2. QCD (Qualified Charitable Distributions)

3. CRT (Charitable Remainder Trust

All three provide benefits depending on how much you want to give. If you want to learn more about this, please send us an email at info@swp360.com.

Estate Planning is another important factor that also needs some attention when building a retirement plan.

Many people who come to see me have no will in place, which poses a problem as everyone needs a will to name powers of attorney. You have to have something in place that tells the financial company who has powers of attorney when it comes to your money.

For instance, I had a client's son call me to let me know his mom was in hospice. He needed $16,000 sent to him to pay for hospice, which wasn't true as Medicare does pick that up. However, the point is, I couldn't send him the money, and nor would Charles Schwab (Custodian) send him the money. The son needed to be listed as the *power of attorney* in order for Schwab to send the money to a name that didn't match the name on the account.

We needed to know who had the power of attorney for his mother's money. Since she didn't have a will, we couldn't transfer him any amount until he got permission from a court. So not everyone needs a trust, but you do need a will. You want to make sure your estate is in order. Doing this would avoid fights among the family, especially concerning assets like jewelry, cars, entertainment systems, gold bars in the safe, etc.

Many low-cost options are available to get a simple will made, and you don't always have to see an expensive attorney. However, we sometimes do need an attorney, depending on the client's situation.

So you see, there is no one size fits all answer, and that's why finding the right financial advisor is so important. As things constantly change depending on new laws, your plan will need to be consistently updated and managed. Dividends get cut, annuities change their rates, tax laws change, healthcare costs are constantly in flux, and what happened yesterday will be very different from what happens tomorrow. Building plans based on what happened yesterday doesn't help anyone.

I have many people who want to see how our portfolios did in 2008. I ask them, "how does that help you"? What happened in 2008 doesn't help you plan for tomorrow's unknown. We need a plan to get you through whatever tomorrow brings. This is the whole reason for building the Retirement Paycheck, as your retirement income is the heartbeat of your retirement. That income allows you to spend the money when you want to spend it. Whether it is on traveling, grandkids, updating your homes, or a new car or boat, that Retirement Paycheck has to be there no matter what.

It would be impossible for me to guarantee that paycheck, even with an annuity (the guarantee from an insurance company is only as good as the claims-paying ability of the insurance company), the plan will need constant attention and management.

Things have changed a lot since I started writing this book in early 2022. This is why flexibility is very important when building the Retirement Paycheck. Interest rates have increased significantly, making fixed annuities, bank CDs, and laddered bond strategies more attractive. Today, you can buy a 5% fixed annuity for 5 years. Also, if the goal was to live on 4%, this would work well through the first 5 years of retirement as you can get it guaranteed and reinvest 1% every year. There is no management fee to the advisor for this type of plan. Individual bonds are also becoming more attractive as bonds mature at par value. This takes away the volatility of the markets and allows you to keep your money while collecting the paycheck. Again, there is no right or wrong way to do this, but you need to have flexibility since we don't know what is going to happen in the future.

This is why you pay your financial advisor.

***

I end this book in the hopes that it has provided you with some guidance on how you can build your Retirement Paycheck. If you have any queries, you can always reach out to me for help at info@swp360.com.

Thank you for reading my book!

-Stephen Smith

Made in the USA
Monee, IL
01 May 2024